A SHORT

HEBREW GRAMMAR

WITHOUT POINTS.

BY SAMUEL SHARPE,

Author of "The History of Egypt."

להבין משל ומליצה
דברי חכמים וחידתם:
Proverbs i. 6.

Wipf & Stock
PUBLISHERS
Eugene, Oregon

Wipf and Stock Publishers
199 W 8th Ave, Suite 3
Eugene, OR 97401

A Short Hebrew Grammar without Points
By Sharpe, Samuel
ISBN 13: 978-1-55635-129-7
ISBN: 1-55635-129-1
Publication date 12/11/2006
Previously published by Samuel Bagster, 1867

PREFACE.

HEBREW is a simple rude language, and one of the easiest for a beginner to read and understand in the narrative parts of the Bible, or indeed in any part when he has the translation open before him. But such is the variety of possible meanings which a word will sometimes bear that it is one of the most difficult languages for an experienced scholar to translate with certainty. It has no auxiliary verbs, such as those by which exactness is gained in English; and has but few inflexions, by which the same exactness is gained in Greek. Even when it was a living language it could not have enabled a speaker to express himself with the logical precision of our own language; and when the speakers reduced their words to writing, they made it yet more obscure by using fewer letters than we should think necessary, and often by the omission of all vowels.

This difficulty later editors of the Scriptures have endeavoured to remove by the introduction of the vowel points, or marks added to the letters to supply the necessary vowels. It is generally acknowledged that these points were not added until after A.D. 700, or shortly before A.D. 1000. About that time the grammatical study of the language flourished among the Jews, and Grammars were written; the introduction of the points led to the need of Grammars suited to the pointed text.

The simplicity of the language, and the use of the points may be explained by examples of doubtful passages. Thus in Psalm xlii. 5, 6 (6, 7), פָּנָיו אֱלֹהִי *of his countenance. O my God*, may be read as פָּנַי וֵאלֹהָי *of my countenance, and my God*. In Ps. lxxxi. 5 (6) שָׂמוֹ, in the Authorised Version *this he ordained*, may be *his name*. In Job xxxvii. 6 עֹזוֹ may be either *his strength*, or *be ye violent*. This uncertainty the Jewish scholars, about the year A.D. 900, undertook to remove by adding the vowel points, which further allowed them to read the scriptures aloud, with a better chance of being understood. But the Jews always scrupulously avoided adding the points to the sacred rolls used in the synagogues.

Against the use of the points it may be said that if we accept their guidance we may be sometimes misled by them. Nor do they give any real help to the thoughtful scholar; for after looking to the points we then have to consider whether they have been rightly placed. And further, if we rely upon them we shall certainly be overlooking some questions which are most important towards rightly understanding the language; namely, by what methods, or arrangement of the words, did the writers mean us to know the exact meaning of a word so insufficiently spelt; or were they in their minds so inexact as sometimes to think it of no importance which of several meanings the reader should give to it.

The Hebrew people were imaginative, poetic, eloquent, and fond of exaggeration; and also unscientific, and careless of accuracy. We, on the other hand, are more prosaic and more exact; and we are apt to look for exactness where it is not to be found. The introduction of the vowel points into the text of the Bible gives a misleading appearance of modern Western accuracy to an ancient Asiatic book.

Our knowledge of the past we owe mainly to tradition. In the case of the Hebrew Scriptures that traditional knowledge has been preserved for us in the Greek translation of the Septuagint, in the Latin Vulgate, in the Jewish commentaries, in the vowel points, and in the more modern kindred languages, such as the Arabic. All these must be studied by those who would gain for themselves a thorough knowledge of the Hebrew language. But they are not necessary for a beginner. He may accept the knowledge derived from those sources as it is embodied for his use in our best Dictionaries and translations. But if he wishes to read the original writings he must read them as they were written without points.

The first scholar who after the revival of learning proposed to reject the vowel points, which the Jews had added to their scriptures, was Bulæus, who in 1658 published his *Methodus Hebraica* at Utrecht. He was followed by Masclef, who published his *Grammatica Hebraica, a Punctis aliisque inventis Massorethicis libera*, at Paris in 1716. His work raised much controversy; it was made known to English readers by Parkhurst, who added a grammar without points to his lexicon; and though many scholars have adopted Masclef's opinion of the little worth of the points, except as a commentary, and for the power of reading aloud, yet the best grammarians and lexicographers have naturally followed the Jews in using them, as they thereby explain the text and the commentary at the same time.

The following pages are founded upon Masclef's Grammar;

and also upon Gesenius's Grammar with the rejection of those parts which relate to the points. Though far from being all that is wanted, they may be useful to beginners, and also to those who, like the writer, think the Massoretic points should be looked at simply as a modern commentary, and who may think them, if used otherwise, rather a hindrance than a help towards gaining a true insight into the Hebrew mind as the writers display it in the Scriptures.

The student who rejects the points will not find himself at all troubled by their presence in books which retain them; except indeed that in some Lexicons words beginning with שׁ are divided into two classes; and accordingly there are two places in such a Lexicon where such a word must be looked for.

The few pages of Chaldee in the Bible, to which of course this Grammar is not fitted, are Ezra iv. 8–vi. 18; vii. 12–26; Daniel ii. 4–vii.; Jeremiah x. 11.

S. S.

32, Highbury Place.
August 20, 1876.

*** A few short notes at the bottom of the page, and a larger one in p. 40, On the Syntax, have been added by a friend of the Publishers.

CONTENTS.

PREFACE	i
The Alphabet	1
THE NOUNS	4
Cases of Nouns	6
The Construct State	6
Irregular Nouns	7
Adjectives	8
Cardinal Numbers	9
Ordinal Numbers	10
THE PRONOUNS.	
Personal Pronouns	11
Demonstrative Pronouns and the Article	13
Relative Pronouns	14
Interrogative Pronouns	14
THE VERB.	
The Conjugations	15
Unusual Conjugations	17
Moods and Tenses	18
The Infinitive Mood	18
The Participles	19
The Imperative Mood	20
The Indicative Mood and its Tenses	20
The Substantive Verb	

CONTENTS.

THE VERB (*continued*).

    Table of a Regular Verb 26
    Irregular Verbs 28
    Verbs Doubly Irregular . . . 31
    Of finding the Root 32

THE PARTICLES.

    Prepositions 33
    The use of את 34
    The Suffix ה 35
    Conjunctions 35
    Adverbs 38
    Interjections 39

A note on the Syntax 40
Grammatical Exercises 40
The Poetry 50
The Prose 52
The Oratory 54
Appendix 57

CORRIGENDA.

THE Author asks the reader to correct the following oversights with his pen.

In page 29, lines 15-17, Verbs in Pe Nun drop the נ in every case in Kal, Hiphil, and Hophal, when the verb takes a formative letter at the beginning, and also in the imperative and infinitive of Kal. They are only regular in Niphal, Hithpael, and in the past tense of Kal.

In page 43, last line, *read,* Niphal of יחר.

In page 49, line 6, *read,* sing. fut. Niph. of נחק.

,,   ,,   ,, 10, *read,* infin. Niphal of זהר.

ALPHABET.

NAME		FORM	FORM AT THE END OF A WORD	SOUND	NUMERAL VALUE
Aleph		א		a	1
Beth		ב		b	2
Gimel	R	ג		g	3
Daleth	R	ד		d	4
He		ה		e, he, h	5
Vau		ו		u, v	6
Zain	R	ז		z	7
Heth or Cheth	R	ח		h, ch	8
Teth	R	ט		t, th	9
Yod		י		i, y, j	10
Caph		כ	ך	k	20
Lamed		ל		l	30
Mem		מ	ם	m	40
Nun		נ	ן	n	50
Samech	R	ס		s	60
Ain or Oin	R	ע		a, o, nasal	70
Pe	R	פ	ף	p, ph	80
Tsaddi	R	צ		ts	90
Quoph	R	ק		q, k	100
Resh	R	ר		r	200
Shin		ש		s, sh	300
Tau		ת		t, th	400

A SHORT
HEBREW GRAMMAR
WITHOUT POINTS.

OF THE LETTERS.

HEBREW is read from the right hand to the left; the reader follows what may be called the backs of the letters. The letters are twenty-two in number, as in the preceding table, to which are added their names, their probable force, as supposed by those who reject the vowel points, and their value as numerals.

The names of the Hebrew letters have been preserved in the Greek alphabet in forms perhaps nearer to the originals. Thus from תו *a mark*, we have ב־תו *B-mark*, or *Beta*; ז־תו, or *Zeta*; ה־תו, or *Eta*; ט־תו, or *Theta*; י־תו, or *Iota*. Other names may have had a preposition before the word תו, as ד־ל־תו, or *Delta*; א־ל־תו, or *Alpha*; ג־מ־תו, or *Gamma*; כ־מ־תו, or *Kappa*; ל־מ־תו, or *Lambda*; ש־מ־תו, or *Sigma*. From these the present Hebrew names seem to have been changed, in order to describe objects which the letters have been thought to represent.

Five of the letters may be read as vowels; and in words which have no written vowel, the reader must supply a short vowel sound to enable him to pronounce the word.

The order of the letters may be learnt from the alphabetic Psalms xxxvii., cxi., cxii., cxix.; and the Lamentations.

Ps. xxv., xxxiv., and cxlv. are also alphabetic, but are defective in the alphabet.

The letters are never used as numerals in the text of the Bible; but they are employed in the margin to number the chapters and verses.[1]

The letters are often divided into radicals and serviles. The eleven letters to which an R is added in the table are radicals. The radicals always form part of the root-word, and are never used for prefixes or suffixes, or the grammatical inflexions, except in one case when ט is used for ת. The other eleven letters are serviles, and are used as prefixes, suffixes, or in the inflexions; but they also sometimes form part of the root. Three of these, ב, ל, and שׁ, scarcely deserve the name of serviles, as they are not used in the inflexions.

A Hebrew word, when we put aside its inflexions and affixes, usually consists of three letters. Such a word is called a root, and in verbs is the third person singular of the past tense. But some roots have only two letters; and some few have four.

Hebrew words may be divided into nouns, pronouns, verbs, and particles, such as prepositions, conjunctions, adverbs, and interjections.

OF NOUNS.

Nouns are usually divided into substantives and adjectives; but the division is less marked in Hebrew than in some other languages.

Nouns are either masculine, or feminine, or common to either gender. Thus בקר *a bull* or *cow*, נער *a boy* or *girl*, are of either gender.

---

[1] In the use of letters as numerals the number 15 is expressed by טו, and not יה, to avoid the form of the divine name Jah; so also 16 is sometimes written טז, because יו is a contraction of יהוה.

OF NOUNS.

Feminine nouns are often known by the termination in ה or ת, as צדקה *righteousness*, אגרת *an epistle*, גפרית *sulphur*.

Masculine nouns usually form the plural in ים, as מלך *a king*, מלכים *kings*. Feminine plural nouns usually end in ות, as מלכה *a queen*, מלכות *queens*.

Feminine nouns which do not end in ה form their plural on the same plan; as ארץ *land*, ארצות *lands*; חרב *a sword*, חרבות *swords*. The ו is not unfrequently omitted.

Masculine nouns ending in ה either form their plural as if feminine, or else drop that letter in the plural, as שדה *a field*, שדות and שדים *fields*. Those ending in י more often drop that letter in the plural; or rather the two Yods coalesce into one, as גוי *a nation*, גויים and גוים *nations*; כלי *vessel*, pl. כלים.

Sometimes Hebrew masculine nouns form their plural as Chaldee nouns, by adding ין in place of ים, as מלכין *kings*, Prov. xxxi. 3.

Several masculine nouns plural end in ות like the feminines, as אבות *fathers;* and several feminine nouns end in ים, as נשים *wives*. Some nouns form their plural in both forms, and without any change of gender, as עצם *a bone*, עצמים and עצמות *bones*. Some again take the double form, as במה *a high place*, במותים *high places*, Deut. xxxii. 13.

The plural form of a noun, when no numeral is added, sometimes must be taken as the dual; thus יומים *days*, meaning *two days*, Exod. xvi. 29; Numb. xi. 19.[1]

Nouns are sometimes put in the plural to strengthen their meaning, as דם *blood*, דמים *bloodshed*, אלהים *God*, אדנים *a lord*, Isa. xix. 4.

So the double plural is used for greater strength, as in the name of Cushan Rishathaim, כושן רשעתים, Judg. iii. 8;

---

[1] Some few nouns singular in sense are only plural in form, as מים *water* חיים *life*, פנים *face*, צהרים *noon*.

from רִשְׁעָה *wickedness*, we have רִשְׁעָתִים *most wicked*, using the genitive of the substantive as an adjective.[1]

Some collective nouns do not take a plural form, as בקר *an ox*, and *oxen;* צאן *sheep* or *goats*. Other nouns are sometimes used as collective, as אבן *stones*, Ex. xxviii. 17. So אלף *a thousand*, and מאה אלף *a hundred thousands*, 2 Chron. xxv. 6. And in the same place, גבור *warriors*.

OF THE CASES OF NOUNS.

Hebrew nouns have no proper cases. Their place is in part supplied by prepositions. The genitive case of other languages is in Hebrew supplied to a noun by its position as following another noun, without its undergoing any change; as רוח אלהים *the breath of God*. The accusative is often marked by the particle את, as, "In the beginning God created, את ה־שמים, the heavens," or "that the heavens." But את does not always mark the accusative; it may rather be said to mark the objective. Its various uses will be explained hereafter.

OF THE CONSTRUCT STATE OF A NOUN.

When a noun is followed by a second noun in the genitive case, although that second noun shows no change, as in Latin and Greek, yet the former noun, which puts it into the genitive, is in some cases changed, and is then said to be *in regimine*, or in the construct state. Thus nouns masculine plural drop the final ם, as מלכי ארץ *kings of the land*, for מלכים ארץ. Feminine nouns singular change the ה into ת, as תורת יהוה *the law of Jehovah*, for תורה יהוה. This change however does not always take place, as in טורים אבן

---

[1] This termination is also used to indicate the dual number, Ex. xxv. 10, אמתים וחצי *two cubits and a half;* Gen. xlv. 6, זה שנתים *these two years*.

rows of stones, Exod. xxviii. 17. A pronoun suffix also puts a noun into the construct state, as דבריך *thy words*, דברי *my words*, or *my word*.

On the other hand this change is sometimes made as it would seem unnecessarily, when the noun is followed by an adjective, as מי ה מרים *bitter waters*, Numb. v. 18. But in such cases we may perhaps understand the adjective as used for a substantive, and translate *waters of bitterness*.[1]

It will be observed that the change we have been describing takes place in the noun which governs, not as in Latin and Greek in the noun which is governed.

A noun is also sometimes put in the construct state, when the second noun is not in the genitive, but is governed by a preposition, as שמחת ב קציר *joy in the harvest*, Isaiah ix. 3 (2).

When two nouns are so united, and express but one complex idea, the descriptive word which follows belongs to the first noun, not to the last, as " Joiada the son of Eliashib, the high priest," Nehem. xiii. 28 ; it is the former, not the latter, to whom the title of high priest belongs.

For the same reason a pronoun suffix is put on the second of two words, as הר קדשי *my holy mountain*.

A LIST OF IRREGULAR NOUNS.

אב *father*, becomes אבי in construct state, or when it receives a suffix, as אביך *thy father*, pl. אבות.

אח *brother*, becomes אחי with a suffix, or when construct.

אחד *one* (once חד), feminine אחת, pl. אחדים *some*.

אחות *sister*, pl. אחיות (as if from אחיה).

איש *man*, pl. seldom אישים, usually אנשים (as from אנש).

---

[1] The genitive to a construct word is often itself construct to another genitive, as in Gen. xxv. 7, ימי שני חיי אברהם *the days of the years of the life of Abraham*.

אמה *maidservant*, pl. אמהות.
אשה *woman*, pl. נשים (as from אנשה).
בית *house*, pl. בתים.
בן *son*, construct once בני, thrice בנו.
בת *daughter*, pl. בנות (as from בנה).
חם *father-in-law;* when it receives a suffix חמי; fem. חמות.
יום *day,* dual יומים, pl. ימים.
מים *water,* construct state מי and מימי.
עיר *city,* pl. ערים (as from ער).
פה *mouth,* construct state פי.

OF ADJECTIVES.

The Hebrew language has but few adjectives; and the want is supplied by substantives in the genitive case. Thus כלי כסף *vessels of silver,* for *silver vessels;* ארון עץ *an ark of wood;* אחזת עולם *a possession for ever.* So איש דברים *a man of words;* בעל שער *an owner of hair,* for *a hairy man;* בן חיל *a son of valour,* or *a valiant man;* בן קדם *a son of the East;* בן שנה *the son of a year,* or *one year old;* בן מות *a son of death, one doomed to die;* בת בליעל *a daughter of Belial,* or *a wicked woman.* So in the New Testament, ὁ κριτης της αδικιας *the judge of injustice,* for *the unjust judge,* Luke xviii. 6.

Adjectives are made feminine by the addition of ה, as טוב *good,* fem. טובה.

An adjective usually stands after the substantive, and agrees with it in gender and number, as ארץ טובה *good land,* ערים גדלת *great cities;* but by no means always.

Sometimes an adverb is used for an adjective, as מ פחד פתאם *from sudden fear,* Prov. iii. 25.

There is no comparative form of the adjective; the thought

is gained by the help of the preposition מ *from;* thus טובה חכמה מ פנינים *good is wisdom above precious stones,* Prov. viii. 11. The superlative is expressed by the word מאד *very*, as טוב מאד *very good;* and sometimes by doubling the adjective, as טוב טוב, Judg. xi. 25.

THE CARDINAL NUMBERS.

FEMININE.		MASCULINE.
אחת	one	אחד
שתים	two	שנים
שלש	three	שלשה
ארבע	four	ארבעה
חמש	five	חמשה
שש	six	ששה
שבע	seven	שבעה
שמנה	eight	שמנה
תשע	nine	תשעה
עשר	ten	עשרה
אחת עשרה / עשתי עשרה	eleven	אחד עשר / עשתי עשר
שתים עשרה	twelve	שנים עשר
שלש עשרה	thirteen	שלשה עשר
ארבע עשרה	fourteen	ארבעה עשר
חמש עשרה	fifteen	חמשה עשר
שש עשרה	sixteen	ששה עשר
שבע עשרה	seventeen	שבעה עשר
שמנה עשרה	eighteen	שמנה עשר
תשע עשרה	nineteen	תשעה עשר

Here it will be observed that the numbers from three to ten, when masculine have a feminine termination, and when feminine have a masculine termination, with one exception.

All the following are of either gender, and from thirty to ninety it will be seen that the plural form means *tenfold*.

עשרים	twenty
שלשים	thirty
ארבעים	forty
חמשים	fifty
ששים	sixty
שבעים	seventy
שמנים	eighty
תשעים	ninety
מאה	a hundred
מאתים	two hundred
שלש מאות	three hundred

and so forth.

אלף	a thousand
אלפים	two thousand
שלש אלף	three thousand

and so forth.

רבבה	ten thousand.[1]

THE ORDINAL NUMBERS.

FEMININE.		MASCULINE.
ראשונה	first	ראשון
שניה and שנית	second	שני
שלישית	third	שלישי

and so forth up to the tenth. For the higher cardinal numbers the ordinal numbers are used.

---

[1] Numerals whose form is that of the singular number are construed with nouns plural, as ארבע כנפים *four wings*, Ezek. x. 21; and those of a plural form take a noun singular, עשרים עיר *twenty cities*, 1 Kings ix. 11; חמש שנים ושׁשׁים שנה *five years and sixty years*, Gen. v. 15.

OF THE PRONOUNS.

The pronouns are either personal, demonstrative, relative, or interrogative.

THE PERSONAL PRONOUNS.

These are used in three forms, as shown in the following table.

1st. Separate, as the nominative to a verb.

2nd. Suffixed to a noun, as the genitive, or as a possessive pronoun.

3rd. Suffixed to a verb, usually as the accusative.

NOMINATIVE.		GENITIVE, AS A SUFFIX.		ACCUSATIVE, AS A SUFFIX.	
I, m. and f.	אנכי אני	*My*, m. and f.	־י	*Me*, m. and f.	־ני
Thou, m.	אתה (את)	*Thy*, m. and f.	־ך	*Thee*, m. and f.	־ך (־ךְ)
Thou, f.	את (אתי)			*Him*	־ו ־הו
He	הוא	*His*	־הו ־ו		(־ה) ־נהו ־נו
She	היא	*Her*	־ה	*Her*	־ה ־נה
We, m. and f.	אנחנו (נחנו) (אנו)	*Our*, m. and f.	־נו	*Us*, m. and f.	־נו
Ye, m.	אתם	*Your*, m.	־כם	*You*, m.	־כם
Ye, f.	אתנה אתן	*Your*, f.	־כן	*You*, f.	־כן
They, m.	המה הם	*Their*, m.	־הם ־ם ־מו	*Them*, m.	(־הם) ־ם ־מו
They, f.	הנה הן	*Their*, f.	־הן ־ן	*Them*, f.	(־הֶן)

Those forms which are within brackets are rare.

With nouns plural the genitive suffix often takes י before it, as מזבחתיך *thine altars*, 1 Kings xix. 10.

הוא *he*, when doubled becomes *this one* and *that one*; thus Zech. vi. 13, "And *this one* shall build the temple of Jehovah; and *that one* shall bear honour; and *he* shall sit and rule upon his throne; and *he* shall be a priest upon his throne. And the counsel of peace shall be between the two."[1]

The Hebrew language has no distinct reciprocal pronouns. The same word represents *him* and *himself*, *his* and *his own*, *them* and *themselves*, *their* and *their own*. Thus in 2 Kings iii. 27 we may read, "he took his own eldest son," or "his eldest son," meaning the Edomite's son.

When the suffix, י *my*, is joined to a plural noun ending in י, the two Yods coalesce into one, as דברי *words*, or *my words*.

Though the pronoun suffix to a verb is usually to be considered as the accusative, yet it is not always so; and the following examples will show an irregularity in that matter:

Psalm v. 4 (5), ינרך *he will dwell with thee*.

Jerem. x. 20, יצאוני *they are gone forth from me*.

  ,,   xx. 7, חזקתני *thou art stronger than I*.

Nehem. ix. 28, יזעקוך *they cried unto thee*.

Psalm xciv. 20, היחברך *shall it have fellowship with thee?*

  ,,   xlii. 4 (5), אדדם *I walked humbly with them*.

Isaiah lxv. 5, קדשתיך *I am holier than thou*.

  ,,   xxxv. 1, ישׂשׂום *they shall be glad for them*.

---

[1] Throughout the Pentateuch the pronoun הוא is generally common in gender, as הוא נתנה לי *she gave to me*, Gen. iii. 12.

The personal pronoun becomes a demonstrative by the prefixture of the article, as בעת ההיא *at that time*, גוים ההם *those nations*.

Psalm liii. 5 (6), חנך *he that encampeth against thee.*
„ cxxxix. 20, יאמרוך *they speak against thee.*
Gen. xxxvii. 4, דברו *to speak to him.*
Exod. xv. 7, קמיך *they that rise up against thee.*
Numb. xi. 23, היקרך *whether it will happen unto thee.*
Isaiah xliv. 21, תנשני *thou shalt be forgotten by me.*

So the suffix to a noun sometimes means the object, as חמסי not *my wrong doing*, but *the wrong done to me*, Jerem. li. 35; יראתו not *his fear*, but *the fear of him*, Exod. xx. 20; and in Job iii. 10, "It shut not the doors of (בטני) the womb for me."

THE DEMONSTRATIVE PRONOUNS, AND THE ARTICLE.

Sing. m.	*This*	זה	and rarely זו.[1]
f.	„	זאת	
Plur.	*These*	אלה	rarely האל.
Article	*The*	ה	prefixed to a noun.

When an adjective accompanies a substantive, the article is often joined to the adjective, as יום ה ששי *the sixth day*; מעשה יהוה ה גדול *the great work of Jehovah*; and sometimes to both substantive and adjective, as ה־עיר ה גדלה *the great city*. The article thus following its noun has the force of a relative pronoun, as הר ה אלהים *a mount, that which is of God*, 1 Kings xix. 8; עמך ה נמצאו פה *thy people, those who are found here*, 1 Chron. xxix. 17.[2]

---

[1] זו is sometimes demonstrative, but more frequently relative, Ex. xv. 13, עם זו גאלת *the people whom thou hast redeemed;* Isa. xlii. 24, זו חטאנו לו *against whom we have sinned.*

[2] A word in construction, or governing a genitive, although itself definite does not take the article, Gen. xlii. 30, האיש אדני הארץ *the man, the lord of the land;* Joel iii. 4, יום יהוה הגדול *the great day of Jehovah.* Similarly a pronoun suffix to a definite noun excludes the article, ידו החזקה *his strong hand*, Deut. xi. 2; as also the prefix ב or ל, בדרך הזה *in this way*, Gen. xxviii. 20.

THE RELATIVE PRONOUNS.

Who, which	אשר [1]	
	שׁ	as a prefix.
Who	מי	rarely.
Which	מה	rarely.

The contraction of the pronoun אשר into שׁ is explained by our finding in the Phenician inscription on the sarcophagus of king Eshmonezer, the intermediate word אשׁ, *who* or *which*, used several times. In the Bible שׁ is met with chiefly in Ecclesiastes and Solomon's Song.[2]

The pronoun מי must be taken as a relative, not as an interrogative, in Jonah i. 8, "Tell us, we pray thee, (באשר למי) *because of whom* this evil is come upon us; What is thine occupation?"

INTERROGATIVE PRONOUN.

Who	of persons	מי
Why, which,	of things	מה

The pronoun מה *which*, is sometimes used for *Whatever;* thus Job xiii. 13, "Let come on me *whatever* will." So, as it is also used adverbially as *Why?* and *How?* it in the same way drops its interrogative force, and means *However;* as Job xix. 28, "Truly ye will say, *However*, we will persecute him." So in the same way the compound interrogative מדוע *why?* bears the same meaning in Job xxiv. 1, "*However*, times are not hidden from the Almighty."

---

[1] The relative אשר is of both genders and numbers, and forms its cases by union with those of the personal pronoun; Ezek. xxxvii. 25, הארץ אשר ישבו בה *the land in which they dwelt*, lit., *which they dwelt in it*. It is often omitted, as Gen. xv. 13, בארץ לא להם *in a land which is not theirs*.

אשר is frequently used as a conjunction, like the Greek ὅτι *that;* Deut. iv. 40, אשר ייטב לך *that it may be well with thee*.

[2] It is found in Judg. v. 7; vi. 17; בשלמי, Jon. i. 7; and, as some think, in the compound word בשגם, *i.e.*, באשר גם, Gen. vi. 3.

OF THE VERB.

The Hebrew verb has several conjugations, which are derivative or allied verbs. It has the indicative mood, the imperative mood, and the infinitive mood, with an active and a passive participle. It has two tenses; one past, and one indefinite, often called the future. It has a singular number and a plural number, with a masculine gender and a feminine gender.

But when we use these names, borrowed from the grammars of Western languages, it must be remembered that the word Conjugation is used in a very different sense, and that the word Tense, as meaning time, is very little applicable to the Hebrew language.

THE CONJUGATIONS.

The chief Hebrew conjugations are five, as follows:

1. KAL.

The conjugation Kal is of the simplest form, and usually a verb active, as קטל *to kill*, פקד *to visit*. But it is often used as a passive verb also, with nothing but the context to guide us as to its force. Thus Isaiah xxiv. 5, "They have changed (חלפו) the statute;" and Psalm cii. 26 (27), "They shall be changed (יחלפו)." Again, Isaiah xli. 15, "Thou shalt beat small (תדק);" and Deut. ix. 21, "It was made small (דק)." Again, Exod. xl. 34, "The glory of Jehovah filled (מלא) the tabernacle;" and 2 Sam. vii. 12, "When thy days shall be fulfilled (ימלאו)."

2. NIPHAL.

This and the following conjugations are named from the forms of פעל, the old example of a Hebrew verb. This conjugation, as its name tells us, is formed by prefixing the letter נ to the past tense. In the other parts of the verb the נ gives way to the inflexion; and then Niphal in form, as in meaning, is the same as Kal.

In its force Niphal is usually the passive of Kal; but sometimes it is reflective, like the Middle Voice of the Greek grammar. Thus 2 Sam. xx. 10, "Amasa did not take heed (נשמר) of the sword;" 1 Sam. xx. 6, "David asked for himself (נשאל)."

3. HIPHIL.

The conjugation Hiphil has two characteristics; first ה added at the beginning, and secondly י inserted before the last letter of the root. The ה, however, like the נ in Niphal, is dropped when the verb takes an inflexion at the beginning. The י is also dropped from the first and second persons of the past tense, and sometimes from the other parts of the verb. The active participle takes מ instead of the ה at the beginning.

In force Hiphil is causative, or doubly active, as ברח *he fled*, הבריח *he made to flee;* שכב *to lie down*, השכיב *to make to lie down*.

But there are some active verbs in which Kal and Hiphil bear the same meaning, as שלך and השליך, *he cast*. And there are some in which Kal and Hiphil are equally intransitive, as שכל and השכיל, *he was wise*, as well as *he made wise*.

This Hebrew form of thought sometimes appears in the New Testament; thus ηὔξανεν, literally, *he increased*, in 1 Cor. iii. 6, means, *he made to increase*. So ἀνατέλλει, literally, *he riseth*, is used in Matth. v. 45 as if it were the Hiphil of the verb, "who maketh his sun to rise."

4. HOPHAL.

The conjugation Hophal is the passive of Hiphil, from which it differs in form only by the omission of the י before the last letter in the root, while it keeps the ה at the beginning in the past tense. But Hophal, like Niphal, sometimes has the force of Kal, as מהלכים *walking*, Eccl. iv. 15.

5. HITHPAEL.

The mark of this conjugation is its receiving the prefix הת to every tense, except when it also receives an inflexion at the beginning, in which case the ה is dropped.

When the first radical of the verb is sibilant, whether ס, צ, or ש, this letter changes place with the ת, as for התשמר is written השתמר; for התסבל is written הסתבל. With צ moreover the ת is usually changed to ט, as for התצדק is written הצטדק. This is the single case in which ט is used as a servile. To this rule there is one exception in התשוטטנה, Jerem. xlix. 3.

In signification Hithpael is reflective, as התקדש *to sanctify one's self*, התאזר *to gird one's self*. It sometimes means to make one's self appear so, as התעשר *to show one's self rich*, התברך *to think one's self blessed*. It is usually intransitive, but not always, as יתפשט את ה־מעיל *he strips himself of his garment*, 1 Sam. xviii. 4.

FIVE UNUSUAL CONJUGATIONS.

These are Pilel and Hithpalel, where the last letter is doubled; and Pilpel, where the last two letters are doubled. This doubling the letters marks repetition, or continuance of the action. Hithpoel takes ו after the first radical, as מסתולל *exalting himself*, Exod. ix. 17. Tiphel, in the Bible, is known only in the verb רגל, from which we have תרגל, and in חרה, from which we have תחרה, and perhaps in רנם, from which we have תרנם. The short Phenician inscription of Eshmonezer gives us two examples of the conjugation Tiphel, in תשמע *to hear*, line 6; and תגדל *to enlarge*, line 20, both in the infinitive mood. The force of Tiphel is the same as Hithpael.

THE MOODS AND TENSES.

These in the conjugation Kal, are

INFINITIVE MOOD.

קטול and קטל   *to slay.*

PARTICIPLE ACTIVE, called BENONI.

קטל or קוטל   *slaying.*

PARTICIPLE PASSIVE, called PAOUL.

קטול   *slain.*

IMPERATIVE MOOD.

קטל   *slay thou.*

INDICATIVE MOOD.

Past tense   קטלתי   *I slew.*

Indefinite, called Future   אקטל   *I slay,* or *shall slay.*

Thus the Hebrew verb is strictly the same as the English verb in its simple state without its auxiliaries.

OF THE INFINITIVE MOOD.

The infinitive mood is often treated like a noun, and receives a preposition as a prefix; thus Exod. vi. 10, "God spake to Moses (לאמר), *saying*," literally, *in order to say;* Prov. xiv. 13, "Even (בשחק) *while* (or *in*) *laughing*, the heart is sorrowful."

In the same way the infinitive may receive a pronoun as a suffix; thus Jerem. ii. 35, אמרך על *because of thy saying.*

A verb in the infinitive mood is often joined to the same verb in the indicative in order to strengthen the expression;

as Amos ix. 8, לא השמיד אשמיד *I will not utterly destroy;* Deut. vii. 2, החרם תחרים *thou shalt utterly destroy.* In such a case the infinitive may also stand after the indicative instead of before it.

This expression is sometimes shown in the Greek, as ευλογων ευλογησω σε *blessing I will bless thee,* Heb. vi. 14.

In such a case the longer form of the infinitive is often used, as Gen. xxxvii. 8 (MSS.), המלוך תמלך *wilt thou certainly rule?* The longer form is also used when it is governed by another verb, as Isaiah xlii. 24, לא אבו הלוך *they did not wish to go.*

When this form of words is accompanied with a negative it is often doubtful whether it strengthens or weakens the expression. Thus Lev. vii. 24, אכל לא תאכלהו *ye shall in no wise eat.* But on the other hand, Judg. i. 28, הוריש לא הורישו *he did not wholly drive him out.* So Isaiah xxx. 19, בכו לא תבכה, the Authorised Version renders, *thou shalt weep no more;* but perhaps a better rendering would be, *thou shalt not always weep.* So Exod. xxxiv. 7, נקה לא ינקה, the Authorised Version renders, *that will by no means clear,* or *acquit;* but a better rendering would be, *not wholly acquitting.* The same doubt hangs over this form of words, when it is used in a question.

In a sentence expressive of several acts, sometimes the first verb only has the signs of tense and person, and the later verbs are in the infinitive mood: thus Dan. ix. 5, מרדנו וסור *we have rebelled, and* [we have] *turned away.*

OF THE PARTICIPLES.

The present participle is sometimes used indefinitely of time, as Eccl. i. 7, "All rivers (הלכים) *are going* into the sea." This participle is also used for the past-present, that is, for the then present, Job i. 14, "The oxen (חרשות) were *plowing;*" Job i. 16, "While this one was yet (מדבר) *speaking.*"

The passive participle is often used as an adjective, as נורא *dreadful, to be feared,* Psalm lxxvi. 8.

OF THE IMPERATIVE MOOD.

The imperative mood has no third person. Its want is supplied by the indicative future, which means both *shall* and *will.* Thus Gen. i. 3, "God said, *Let there be* (יהי) light," literally, *there shall be.*

OF THE INDICATIVE MOOD, AND ITS TENSES.

Before entering on the study of the tenses, where we shall meet with many difficulties, it will be well to consider tenses or times in general. This our own language enables us to do by means of its auxiliary verbs. Our indefinite tenses are very nearly the same as the Hebrew, as shown in page 18. Our chief definite tenses are nine, thus:

1. Past-past   *I had visited,* or *been visiting.*
2. Past-present   *I was visiting.*
3. Past-future   *I was about to visit.*

1. Present-past   *I have visited,* or *been visiting.*
2. Present-present *I am visiting.*
3. Present-future   *I am about to visit.*

1. Future-past   *I shall have visited,* or *been visiting.*
2. Future-present   *I shall be visiting.*
3. Future-future   *I shall be about to visit.*

INDICATIVE MOOD.

No such exactness as the above is possible in Hebrew. The last indeed in each of the above triplets we may put aside as not to be looked for in a language of a simple character. The second in each triplet is expressed in Hebrew, as in English, by means of the present participle. And we now proceed to show by examples how the two Hebrew tenses are used, not only for the three indefinite times, but also for three definite times, namely, the first in each of the above triplets.

1st. The future tense used as our future indefinite.
2nd. ,,   ,,   ,,   ,,   present indefinite.
3rd. ,,   ,,   ,,   ,,   past indefinite.
4th. The past tense used as our past indefinite, present-past, and past-past.
5th. ,,   ,,   ,,   ,,   present indefinite.
6th. ,,   ,,   ,,   ,,   future indefinite, and future-past.

1st. The use of the future tense for future time is frequent, and scarcely needs an example; as Joel ii. 19, "Then Jehovah will answer (יען) and will say (יאמר) to his people."

This tense also expresses in the first person a future intention, as Isaiah i. 24, "Ah, I will ease myself (אנחם) of mine adversaries;" and in the other person a command, as in Gen. i. 3, "God said, There shall be (יהי) light," which we translate, "Let there be light."

2nd. Less frequent is the use of this tense for the present time, as 1 Sam. xxi. 14 (15), "Lo, ye see (תראו) the man is mad;" and Psalm xvii. 12, "As a lion that is greedy (יכסוף) of his prey."

3rd. The future tense is often used as the historian's tense for simple narrative, as in English the present tense may be so used; thus 1 Kings iii. 1, "And Solomon joineth himself by marriage (יתחתן) to Pharaoh king of Lower Egypt, and he taketh (יקח) Pharaoh's daughter, and bringeth her (יביאה) into the city of David." Again, Gen. i. 7, "And God maketh (יעש) the firmament, and divideth (יבדל) the waters which were under the firmament from the waters which were above the firmament; and it is (יהי) so." But in an English translation it is more convenient to put these verbs into the past tense.

4th. The Hebrew past tense is used for the simple past in Gen. i. 1, "In the beginning God created (ברא) the heavens and the earth." The historian then continues his narrative in the indefinite or future tense as shown above.

It is also used for the present-past, or preterperfect, as in 1 Sam. xv. 13, "Saul saith to him, Blessed be thou of Jehovah, I have performed (הקימתי) the command of Jehovah."

It is also used for the past-past, or pluperfect, as in Exod. xii. 39, "And they baked unleavened cakes of the dough which they had brought out (הוציאו) of Egypt."

5th. The past tense is used where in English we use the present, when speaking of an habitual act, or habit acquired. Thus in Ps. i. 1, "Blessed is the man that walketh (הלך) not in the counsel of the wicked, nor standeth (עמד) in the way of sinners, nor sitteth (ישב) in the seat of the scornful." Latin and Greek usage here agrees with the Hebrew in such words as Odi *I hate*, Γνωναι *to know*.

This must not, however, lead us to treat as general moral remarks those passages which point to particular acts, such as Isaiah xxxiii. 15, "Who of us shall dwell through everlasting burnings? He that hath walked (הלך) in righteousness, and hath spoken (דבר) uprightly, he that hath refused

(מאס) the gain of oppression, and hath shaken (נער) his hands from taking bribes." The prophet is pointing reproachfully to those Jews who had taken office under their Babylonian conquerors, and had been partners in their tyranny.

6th. Our chief difficulty is with those cases in which we find it necessary to translate a Hebrew past tense by an English future, the difficulty of understanding how the writers could have been satisfied with such, to us, seeming inexactness. Our examples may be classed under several heads.

(a) In some cases a fixed purpose, or intention, like a habit of mind mentioned above, is expressed in a past tense, where the thought is future, but where we in English use a present. Thus in Ruth iv. 3 Boaz says, that Naomi "is selling (מכרה) her land;" that is, she has determined to sell it. In Gen. xxiii. 11, the Hittite says to Abraham, "I give (נתתי) to thee the field;" and Abraham answers, "I will give (נתתי) thee money for the field." So Psalm xx. 6 (7), "Now I know that Jehovah saveth (הושיע) his anointed one." In all these cases the past tense expresses a future act.

This is particularly allowed after an oath, as in 2 Kings v. 20, "As Jehovah liveth, I will run (רצתי) after him, and will take (לקחתי) somewhat from him." So also in words spoken by Jehovah, a promise for the future is naturally spoken of as already performed, as in Jerem. xv. 11, "I will set thee free (שרותיך);" and Lev. xxvi. 44, "I will not cast them away (מאסתים), neither will I abhor them (געלתים)."

So in a prophecy a future event may be spoken of as already seen in the mind's eye. Thus Num. xxiv. 17:—

"I shall see him, but not now;
I shall look round upon him, but not nigh.
There will come (דרך *came*) a star out of Jacob,
And a sceptre will arise (קם *arose*) out of Israel,
And he will smite (מחץ *smote*) the sides of Moab."

But this will not justify our reading past tenses as prophetic, when there are no words pointing to a future time, such as we have in the first two lines of the above.

(*b*) The past tense is not unnaturally used for the future-past, as in Isaiah xi. 9, "They shall not hurt nor destroy in all my holy mountain; for the earth shall be full (מלאה shall have been filled) of the knowledge of Jehovah;" and Lev. xix. 8, "He that eateth shall bear his iniquity, because he hath profaned (חלל, will have profaned) what was holy." So in Jerem. xi. 4, we write, "And ye shall be my people, and I will be your God." But if we would explain the use of the tenses, we must translate more literally, but awkwardly, "And when ye have been (הייתם) my people, then I will be (אהיה) your God."

(*c*) There remains a large class of passages in which a number of future thoughts or actions follow one another; where the writer has been content with using a future tense for the first verb, as if trusting that the verbs which follow will be understood as future, though in the past tense. Thus Jerem. xlvi. 22, "And they shall march with an army, and come (באו) against her with axes;" Jerem. l. 13, "It shall not be inhabited, but shall be (היתה) wholly desolate."

As a good example of the difference between the Hebrew mind and the English in the use of the tenses, take Jerem. vii. 13-15: "And now because ye have done all these works, Jehovah hath said it, and I spake (אדבר *I speak*) to you, rising up early and speaking, but ye heard not, and I called

(אקרא *I call*) to you, but ye answered not; therefore I will do (עשיתי *I have done*) to this house which is called by my name, wherein ye trust, and to the place which I gave to you and to your fathers, as I did to Shiloh. And I will cast (השלכתי *I have cast*) you out of my sight, as I did cast out all your brethren, the whole seed of Ephraim."

In this simple sentence, about the meaning of which there can be no doubt, the reasons given above may be enough to explain why "I spake" and "I called" are in the indefinite narrative or future tense; but it is not easy to find any reason why "I will do" and "I will cast" are in the past tense.

THE SUBSTANTIVE VERB.

The verb היה *to be*, is rarely used as a simple substantive verb. Its place is supplied by the apposition of the two nouns; as יהוה אלהינו *Jehovah* [is] *our God*, Deut. vi. 4; אנכי הראה *I* [am] *the seer*, 1 Sam. ix. 19.

The following table shows a regular verb in its more usual conjugations, with the inflexions which mark its moods, its tenses, its numbers, and its genders:—

EXAMPLE OF A

	TENSE.	PERSONS.	KAL.	NIPHAL.
Indicative Mood.	Past.	3 Sing. m.	קטל	נקטל
		3 f.	קטלה	נקטלה
		2 c.	קטלת	נקטלת
		1 c.	קטלתי	נקטלתי
		3 Plur. c.	קטלו	נקטלו
		2 m.	קטלתם	נקטלתם
		2 f.	קטלתן	נקטלתן
		1 c.	קטלנו	נקטלנו
	Future.	3 Sing. m.	יקטל	
		3 f.	תקטל	
		2 m.	תקטל	
		2 f.	תקטלי	
		1 c.	אקטל	Same as Kal.
		3 Plur. m.	יקטלו	
		3 f.	תקטלנה	
		2 m.	תקטלו	
		2 f.	תקטלנה	
		1 c.	נקטל	
Infinitive Mood.			קטל or קטול	הקטל or נקטל
Imperative Mood.		Sing. m.	קטל	הקטל
		f.	קטלי	הקטלי
		Plur. m.	קטלו	הקטלו
		f.	קטלנה	הקטלנה
Participle Active			קוטל	נקטל
Passive			קטול	

REGULAR VERB.

HIPHIL.	HOPHAL.	HITHPAEL.
הקטיל	הקטל	התקטל
הקטילה	הקטלה	התקטלה
הקטלת	הקטלת	התקטלת
הקטלתי	הקטלתי	התקטלתי
הקטילו	הקטלו	התקטלו
הקטלתם	הקטלתם	התקטלתם
הקטלתן	הקטלתן	התקטלתן
הקטלנו	הקטלנו	התקטלנו
יקטיל		יתקטל
תקטיל		תתקטל
תקטיל		תתקטל
תקטילי		תתקטלי
אקטיל	Same as	אתקטל
יקטילו	Kal.	יתקטלו
תקטלנה		תתקטלנה
תקטילו		התקטלו
תקטלנה		תתקטלנה
נקטיל		נתקטל
הקטיל	הקטל	התקטל
הקטל		התקטל
הקטילי	Wanting.	התקטלי
הקטילו		התקטלו
הקטלנה		התקטלנה
מקטיל		מתקטל
	מקטל	

The participles form their feminine and plural like adjectives.

In the future tense the first person, whether in the singular or in the plural, is sometimes lengthened by an ה at the end. This is done to give strength and emphasis to a command. The third person is sometimes, though rarely, so lengthened, as ירשנה in Psalm xx. 3 (4); יחישה, Isaiah v. 19; and תעגבה, Ezek. xxiii. 20.

The imperative is also so lengthened; and it is then called the cohortative form.

A ן is sometimes added after the ו in the third person masculine plural of the future, and is called paragogic, or additional. In such a case the ו is sometimes dropped, as in יריבן *they strive*, Exod. xxi. 18; ירשיען *they will condemn*, Exod. xxii. 8; and more rarely in the second person masculine plural of the future, as תאריכן *ye shall prolong*, Deut. iv. 26.[1]

The final י in the first person singular of the past is sometimes dropped, as משיתהו *I raised him up*, Exod. ii. 10; הרביתך *I multiply thee*, Gen. xlviii. 4.

The ו in the participles, the י in Hiphil, and the ה in the feminine plural are all sometimes dropped.

IRREGULAR VERBS.

These are of various classes, and they are described by the letters of the exemplar verb פעל. Verbs beginning with

---

[1] Certain other paragogic letters are occasionally added to words either redundantly or with doubtful signification; as א to verbs, Isa. xxviii. 12, (אבו) לא אבוא שמוע *they would not hear;* ו and י to nouns construct, Ps. l. 10, (חית) חיתו יער *the beast of the forest;* Ps. cxiv. 8, (מעין) מעינו מים *a fountain of water;* Lam. i. 1, (רבה) רבתי בגוים *great among the nations;* Ps. cx. 4, (דברה) דברתי על *after the manner.*

either י, or נ, or א, and one with ל, are called defective in Pe Yod, פי, or in Pe Nun, פנ, or in Pe Aleph, פא, or in Pe Lamed, פל.

פי.

Many verbs in Pe Yod, but not all, drop the י in the infinitive, imperative, and future, forming those parts of the verb as if the root had only two letters. Thus from ישב *he dwelt*, we have imperative שב *dwell thou*, and future אשב *I shall dwell*. They sometimes add a ת to the infinitive, שבת *to dwell*. The same verbs in Niphal, Hiphil, and Hophal usually change the י into ו, as הושיב *he made to dwell*. Some few simply drop the י in these conjugations, as from יצת *to be burnt*, Hiphil הצית *he kindled*.

פנ.

Verbs in Pe Nun drop the נ in every case in which the verb takes an inflection at the beginning, and also in the imperative and infinitive of Kal; and are only regular in the past tense of Kal. Thus from נגש *he came near*; infinitive, גשת *to come near*; imperative, גש *do thou come near*; future, אגש *I will come near*; Hiphil, הגיש *he brought near*.

פא.

Verbs in Pe Aleph drop the א in the first person singular of the future of Kal, as אכל *I will eat*, instead of אאכל. They sometimes, though rarely, drop the א in other parts of the verb, as ימרו *they will say*, Ps. cxxxix. 20, instead of יאמרו.

פל.

The verb לקח *he took*, is defective as to the first letter in the infinitive, imperative, and future of Kal; as קח *to take*, and *take thou*; יקח *he will take*.

עו and עי.

Verbs in Ain Vau and Ain Yod, that is, verbs of which the middle letter is either ו or י, usually drop that letter in the past tense of Kal, as from קום *to arise*, קם *he arose;* and in the participle active, קם *arising;* and in Hiphil, הקים *he raised;* and in Hophal, הוקם *he was raised*, and sometimes in the future of Kal, as יקם *he will arise*. Moreover, in the inflections of the past tenses of Niphal and Hiphil, they usually take ו before the formatives of the first and second persons, תי, ת, תם, תן, נו, as in Niphal נקומותי, נקומות, נקומונו, נקומותן, נקומותם, and the same in Hiphil. In Hophal the ו precedes the first radical, as הוקם for הקום, *he was raised*. For the inflection נה in the future they sometimes take ינה as הקומינה, *the women will raise*. Verbs of this form often appear in the less usual conjugation Pilel, with the last letter doubled, as קומם from קום.

עע.

Verbs in Ain doubled, that is with second and third radicals alike, are in many of their parts defective in the same way as verbs in Ain Vau, and moreover like them take a ו before the first radical in Hophal; and for the inflection נה in the future they sometimes take ינה. Thus from סבב we have סב *he went round;* הוסב *he was turned round;* תסבינה *the women will go round*.

לן.

Verbs in Lamed Nun, that is with ן for the last letter, naturally lose that letter when it is followed by an inflection beginning with נ; the two letters coalesce into one.

לת.

Verbs in Lamed Tau, that is those ending with ת, in the

same way lose the letter ת at the end when it is followed by an inflexion beginning with ת; the two letters coalesce into one.

לא.

Verbs in Lamed Aleph sometimes drop the א, as from מצא *he found*, מצתי *I found*, Num. xi. 11. They sometimes change the א into ה, as from רפא *to heal*, imperative רפה *heal thou*, Ps. lx. 4.

לה.

Verbs in Lamed He are usually irregular. They often drop the ה, as from ענה *to be afflicted*, יענו *they will be afflicted*. Before the inflexion ה it is changed into ת, as ענתה *she was afflicted*. Before ת it is changed into י, as ענית *thou wast afflicted*; so also before נ, as תענינה *the women will be afflicted*. In the past participle also the ה is changed into י as ענוי *afflicted*.

VERBS DOUBLY IRREGULAR.

Not a few words ending in א or ה, and beginning with א, י, or נ, are irregular as to both the first and the last letter. Of these verbs the following is a list. Their irregularities are too numerous to be here set forth; they must be learnt by experience.

אבה *he is willing.*	ירא *he feared.*
אוה *he desired.*	יאה *it suited.*
אלה *he swore.*	יגה *he grieved.*
אנה *he lamented.*	ידה *he cast.*
אפה *he baked.*	ינה *he oppressed.*
ארה *he plucked.*	יעה *he swept away.*
אתה *he came.*	יפה *he was fair.*
יצא *he went out.*	ירה *he threw.*

יש *it is.*	נטה *he stretched.*
נאה *it was fit.*	נכה *he smote.*
נדה *he thrust forth.*	נלה *he finished.*
נבא *he prophesied.*	נסה *he tempted.*
נהה *he lamented.*	נצה *he strove.*
נוה *he dwelt.*	נקה *he was pure.*
נזה *he sprinkled.*	נשא *he raised.*
נחה *he led.*	נשה *he forgot,* or *lent.*

There are also a few verbs with four or five letters in the root. They form their tenses regularly.

ON FINDING THE ROOT OF A VERB.

From what has been said about the irregular verbs, it is clear that they will not always be found in the dictionary under the letters met with in a text, even after we have rejected the inflexions at the beginning and at the end.

If after the formative letters have been rejected three letters remain, that is probably the root.

If only two letters remain, that may be the root. But if not, add י or נ, or more rarely א or ל, to the beginning, or insert ו or י in the middle; or add at the end one of the letters which the last class of irregular verbs may have thrown off; or double the last letter.

If, however, only one letter should remain, add י or נ to the beginning and ה to the end.

These rules will generally enable a learner to find the required root in the dictionary.

THE PARTICLES.

The Hebrew particles are Prepositions, together with a suffix having the force of a preposition, Conjunctions, adverbs, and interjections. Some of these are original; but many are compound, formed from other particles and from nouns.

THE PREPOSITIONS.

אל, אלי, ל	*To, towards.*
אצל	*At, near, by the side of.*
אחר, אחרי	*After, behind.*
את, אות	*With,* and sign of objective case.
ב	*In,* before a verb *when.*
בין	*Between.*
בגלל, בשל	*Because of.*
למען	*So that.*
בעד	*For.*
חלף, תחת	*Instead of.*
בכא, בלי, לבלי, מבלי	*Without.*
לבד, מלבד	*Except, alone.*
זולת, זולתי	*Except.*
עבר, מעבר, אל עבר	*Beyond.*
בעבור	*Because of.*
עם, עמד	*With.*
עד, עדי	*Until, during.*
על, עלי	*Upon, over, above.*
תחת	*Instead of, under.*
נגד, נכח, לנכח	*In front of.*
מול, ממול	*Over against.*
מ, מן, מני, למן, למני	*From, a part of, away from.*
סביב	*Around.*

Prepositions take suffixes as nouns; thus אצלי *near me*, תחתי *instead of me*. They also receive prefixes, and thus become compound prepositions, as מעבר.

The Hebrew language has no verbs compounded of pre-

4

positions, like the Latin words prefix and suffix. Such modes of thought are expressed by the prepositions which follow the verb.

The use of the preposition is very various. As an example, the preposition מ in its simplest meaning is *from;* thus 1 Sam. v. 1, "They brought it *from* Eben-ezer to Ashdod." But it often retains somewhat of its original meaning, as מן *a portion;* thus Exod. xvii. 5, "Take with thee *some of* the elders of Israel." Again, Gen. xxvii. 28, "May God give thee *of* the dew of heaven, and *of* the fat of the land." But in Gen. xxvii. 39, with words nearly the same, but following a different verb, this preposition has the very opposite force; thus, "Thy dwelling shall be *apart from* the fat of the land, and *apart from* the dew of heaven." It is in poetry that such violent use of words is chiefly met with. Thus Job xxxv. 3, "What profit shall I have *if free from* my sin?" and xix. 26, "And *apart from* my flesh I shall see God."

The preposition את rarely admits any English meaning. It is usually the mark of the accusative case, as Gen. i. 1, "In the beginning God created את ה־שמים *the heavens.*" It is also sometimes the sign of the nominative to a passive verb, particularly when that nominative is out of its usual place in the sentence, and it might be translated *namely,* as marking the object; thus Gen. iv. 18, "And unto Enoch was born את עירד *namely Irad;*" 2 Sam. xi. 25, "Let it not be evil in thine eyes את ה־דבר ה־זה *namely this* thing;" and 1 Sam. xx. 13, "If it shall be pleasing unto my father את ה־רעה *namely the evil* unto thee." In Josh. xxii. 17 and Nehem. ix. 32 את is used in the same manner. In Gen. iv. 1 it may bear the meaning of *from*, "I have gotten a man *from* Jehovah." In Isaiah xi. 9, דעה את יהוה *knowledge of*

Jehovah, את marks the genitive case, unless we suppose that the noun, like the verb from which it is derived, governs an accusative.

When any more exact meaning is given to את it is usually *with*, as in Num. i. 5; Lev. xix. 13; Judg. xvii. 11. And this has led to some curious mistakes in the Septuagint, where the translator has treated the Greek preposition, συν *with*, as if representing את, and as if συν were simply the sign of the accusative case. Thus Eccl. ii. 17, "I hated life," is rendered εμισησα συν την ζωην; and iii. 17, "The righteous and the wicked, God will judge," is rendered συν τον δικαιον και συν τον ασεβη κρινει ὁ Θεος.

THE SUFFIX ה.

The single suffix with the force of a preposition is

  ה *Towards, unto.*

It may be compared to our English suffix -wards, in homewards, backwards, etc., as אשדודה *to Ashdod*, 1 Sam. v. 1. When this suffix is joined to a word ending in ה, the two letters coalesce into one, as in Ezek. xxix. 10, "From Migdol *to Syene* (סונה), even to the boundary of Ethiopia."

THE CONJUNCTIONS.

  ו *And, but, even, then, when.*
  גם *Also.*
  אף *Also.*
  או *Or.*
  אם *If.*
  כן *Thus, so.*
  כי *Because, for.*
  אלו, לו *If, oh that.*

לוּלָא, לוּלֵי	*If not, unless.*
אַךְ, אֲבָל, אוּלָם	*But, however.*
יַעַן, עֵקֶב	*Because.*
פֶּן	*Lest.*

The meanings which these conjunctions bear are very various. Those of ו need explanation as they bear on the force of the tenses. See page 24.

1. ו *And.*

Often a simple copulative, as Gen. i. 1, "In the beginning God created the heavens *and* the earth."

2. ו *Now.*

It bears this weak force, *now*, at the beginning of a sentence, as Exod. i. 1, "*Now* these are the names of the sons of Israel, who came into Lower Egypt with Jacob;" Deut. iv. 44, "*Now* this is the law which Moses set before the children of Israel;" Esther i. 1, "*Now* it came to pass in the days of Ahasuerus."

3. ו *Even.*

It bears this weak force, *even*, when it unites two words or sentences which have the same meaning, and are placed *in apposition* one to the other; as 1 Sam. vi. 19, "He smote the men of Beth-shemesh, because they looked into the ark of Jehovah, *even* he smote of the people fifty thousand and seventy men;" Zech. ix. 9, "Behold, thy king cometh to thee. He is just, and hath been saved, lowly and riding upon an ass, *even* upon a colt the foal of an ass;" Jerem. xxxii. 9, "And I weighed to him the silver, seven shekels, *even* ten pieces of silver." Perhaps Hos. iii. 2 should be so translated, "I bought her to me for fifteen pieces of silver, *even* for a homer of barley and a lathach of barley."

4. ו *Then, and then.*

This stronger force of ו is often used in narrative, as Nehem. ii. 9, "*Then* I came to the pashas beyond the river;" ii. 17, "*Then* I said to them;" iii. 1, "*Then* Eliashib the high priest rose up."

In this way ו often has an argumentative force; as Job xxii. 21, "Make him thy friend, *and then* be at peace;" Jerem. xiv. 18, "If I go forth into the field, *then* behold, the slain with the sword; and if I enter the city, *then* behold, those who are sick through famine."

We have the same Hebrew use of the word καɩ in Romans i. 16, "To the Jew first, *and then* to the Greek;" Heb. x. 15-17, "For after it was first said, This is the covenant ...; *then*, Their sins and iniquities I will remember no more."

5. ו *But, yet, although.*

Isaiah viii. 9, "Do your worst, O ye peoples, *and yet* ye shall be broken to pieces;" Gen. xviii. 13, "Shall I surely bear a child, *although* I am old."

So καɩ has this force in Eph. iv. 26, "Be angry *and yet* sin not."

6. ו *For.*

As in Ruth i. 21, "Why call ye me Naomi, *for* Jehovah hath testified against me?" Josh. xvii. 14, "Why hast thou given to me as an inheritance one lot, and one portion, *for* I am a great people?"

7. ו—ו, *And when—then.*

This use of ו may help to explain some of the difficulties in regard to the past tense when we in ordinary cases are led to be less literal, and to render it by the future. Thus Jerem. xi. 4, "Obey my voice; *and when* ye have done these things according to all that I command thee, and ye have been my people, *then* I will be your God." Also Jerem. vii. 23, "Obey my voice, *and when* I have been your God (or have been listened to), *then* ye shall be my people."

ADVERBS.

ה	A prefix, the sign of interrogation.
אי, איה, איזה	*Where?*
איך, איכה	*How?*
אין, אל, לא (לו rarely)	*Not.*
איפה	*Where? when?*
איפוא	*So then.*
אן, אין	*Where?*
אנה	*Whither?*
מאן, מאין	*Whence?*
כ	*As.*
פה, פא, פו	*Here.*
מפה, מפו	*Hence.*
זה, בזה, שם	*Here, there.*
כה, הלם	*Thus, here, hither.*
הן, הנה	*Lo, behold, there, here.*
חוץ	*Outside.*
מדוע	*Why, how, however;* see מה, p. 14.
מטה	*Below.*
מתי	*When?*
עד מה, עד אי	*Until when?*
מחר	*Tomorrow.*
תמול	*Yesterday, formerly.*
אמש	*Last night.*

שלשם, שלשום	The day before yesterday.
יומם	By day, daily.
בקר	In the morning.
שחר	At daybreak.
ערב	In the evening.
תמיד	Continually, daily.
נצח, לנצח, לעולם, עד	Always, for ever.
קדם, מקדם, כבר	Of old, formerly.
טרם	Not yet.
מהר, פתאם	Quickly.
רגע	In a twinkling.

To this list many more might be added, which are in frequent use; such as those compounded, by the help of a preposition, from other particles or from nouns.

Adverbs sometimes receive a pronoun suffix, like verbs, as איני *not I;* אינך *not thou.*

The interrogative particle ה is sometimes omitted, and a question is asked without any interrogative sign, as Gen. xxvii. 24, "Art thou my very son Esau?"

INTERJECTIONS.

נא, אנא, אנה, בי	I pray now, now.
אי; אוי, הה, אהה, הו	Alas, oh.
אויה, הוי, אח, אחה	Alas, oh.
אללי	Alas.
חלילה	Far be it, keep off.
האח	Aha.
לו, לוא, אחלי	Oh that, if.
מי יתן	O that, who will give?
אמן	Truly.
הן, הנה	See here, behold.

Interjections, like adverbs, receive a pronoun suffix, as
הנני *here I am*, הננו *here we are*.[1]

GRAMMATICAL EXERCISES.

In the following exercises the parsing of each word is given; its prefix and suffix, when it has such, are treated as separate words. If it is not itself a root-word, its inflexions are explained by the help of the grammar; and it is then referred to a root which may be found in the Lexicon. When a word is met with several times, its explanation is not always

---

[1] NOTES ON SYNTAX.—The Hebrew syntax is by no means strict, and there are many exceptions to all its rules. Of such as have not already been incidentally noticed the following are some of the more noteworthy.

A transitive verb usually governs an accusative case, with or without את, but some verbs are construed with a prefix; ויקרא לאור יום *and He called the light Day;* בחר בי *he chose me.*

Intransitive verbs are sometimes accompanied pleonastically by cognate nouns, חרדו חרדה *they feared (with) fear;* צמו צום *they fasted (kept) a fast.*

The predicate, whether verb or adjective, commonly precedes its subject, and sometimes takes its uninflected form, or one of priority (as masc. for fem.) regardless of the state of the subject, חזק המלחמה *the war increased;* לא נמצא נשים *women were not found;* יצאו בנות *daughters go out.*

If different nouns form the subject, the verb is usually masc. plural, but it may agree with the first one only, ותדבר מרים ואהרן *and Miriam and Aaron spake;* ויפל דוד והזקנים *and David and the elders bowed,* 1 Ch. xxi. 16.

The feminine is used as a neuter, זאת *this thing,* אחת *one thing,* גדולות *great things,* Ps. xxvii. 4; xii. 4; and a fem. plural of things may have a verb singular, like Greek neuters, נשברה דלתות *the gates are broken.*

A verb will sometimes agree with a genitive instead of its construct nominative, ובאו חמדת כל הגוים *and the Desire of all nations shall come;* קול שמועה באה *the sound of a report comes,* Jer. x. 22.

A noun of multitude, as עם *a people,* takes a verb singular or plural.

Nouns of plural form, as מים *water,* שמים *heaven,* are mostly with a verb plural; but a noun used in the plural of eminence, as אלהים, אדנים, commonly has its verb in the singular.

By ellipsis a noun is often used adverbially, Ex. xxiv. 3, *answered (with) one voice;* Gen. xli. 40, *only (in) the throne.* Ellipsis of a repeated negative also often occurs, Ps. ix. 19, *shall (not) perish.*

The nominative absolute is of frequent occurrence, Gen. xxviii. 7, ואני בבואי *and I, in my coming,* etc., *Rachel died.* Somewhat similarly the nominative pronoun occurs after its suffix for emphasis, לכם אתם *to you,*

repeated. If the conjugation of a verb is not given, it may be understood to be Kal. If the gender and number of a noun are not given, it may be understood as masculine singular, or that its gender in that place is not required.

Genesis I. 1–8.

(1) ב *in*, preposit. ראשית *beginning*, noun. ברא *created*, 3 pers. sing. past. אלהים *God*, noun plur. of אלוה; nomin. to sing. verb. את, sign of accusat. ה *the*, article. שמים *heavens*, noun plur. ו *and*, conjunc. את, sign of accusat. ה *the*, article. ארץ *earth*, noun. (2) ו *and*. ה *the*. ארץ *earth*, noun fem. היתה *was*, 3 pers. fem. sing. past of היה. תהו *without form*, noun. ו *and*. בהו *void*, noun. ו *and*. חשך *darkness*, noun, (*was*). על *upon*, prep. פני *face*, noun plur. in construct state for פנים. תהום *of the deep*, noun genit., putting the former into construct state. ו *and*. רוח *breath*, noun fem. אלהים *of God*, genit. by position, (*was*).

even ye; זכרם המה *their memory, even of them.* There is also occasionally a pleonastic use of the dative pronoun, Gen. xii. 1, לך לך *get thee away;* Isa. xxxi. 8, נס לו *he flees for himself.*

The substantive verb is used as in Latin with a dative to denote possession, ללוט היה צאן *Lot possessed flocks.* In like manner יש, Gen. xliv. 20, יש לנו אב *we have a father.*

The dative of becoming or being made is also in common use, Gen. xii. 2, אעשך לגוי גדול *I will make thee a great nation;* Gen. xx. 12, ותהי לי לאשה *and she became my wife.*

Some verbs are used impersonally, as ויצר לו *and it was grievous to him;* ינח לי *it is quiet to me (I am quiet);* ויהי *and it was*, or *happened.* There is also a frequent ellipsis of an indefinite nominative, as Gen. xi. 9, קרא שמה בבל *(one) calls its name Babel;* ויאמר ליוסף *and (one) told Joseph.*

The repetition of nouns usually denotes distribution, as עדר עדר *flock by flock;* but if coupled by ו diversity, אבן ואבן *divers weights.*

In the margin of Hebrew Bibles are given certain notes accompanied by the word קרי. They are generally corrections of apparently grammatical errors in the text, called כתיב, *i.e., written*, which copyists have not ventured to alter, and for which the קרי is to be *read.* Thus 2 Chron. ii. 18, בן marg. בת; Josh. xv. 47, הגבול marg. הגדול. Occasionally, however, some Hebraists do not adopt the Qeri, but prefer the Kethib.

מרחפת *moving*, particip. fem. Hiphil of רחף. על *upon.* פני *face*, noun in construct. ה *the.* מים *waters*, noun plur. genit. by position. (3) ו *then.* יאמר *saith*, 3 pers. sing. fut. of אמר. אלהים *God*, nominat. יהי *there shall be*, 3 pers. sing. fut. for imperative of היה. אור *light*, noun. ו *and.* יהי *there is*, 3 pers. sing. fut. אור *light.* (4) ו *and.* ירא *seeth*, 3 pers. sing. fut. of ראה. אלהים *God*, nominat. את sign of acc. ה *the.* אור *light.* כי *that*, conjunct., (*it is*). טוב *good*, adjec. ו *and.* יבדל *divideth*, 3 pers. sing. fut. of בדל. אלהים *God*, nominat. בין *between*, prepos. ה *the.* אור *light.* ו *and.* בין *between.* ה *the.* חשך *darkness.* (5) ו *and.* יקרא *calleth*, 3 pers. sing. fut. אלהים *God*, nomin. ל *to*, prep. אור *light.* יום *day*, noun. ו *and.* ל *to.* חשך *darkness.* קרא *he called*, 3 pers. sing. past, or infinit. לילה *night*, noun. ו *and.* יהי *there is.* ערב *evening*, noun. ו *and.* יהי *there is.* בקר *morning.* יום *day.* אחד *first*, cardinal for ordinal numb. (6) ו *and.* יאמר *saith.* אלהים *God.* יהי *there shall be.* רקיע *a firmament*, noun. ב *in*, prep. תוך *the middle*, noun. ה *the.* מים *waters*, genit. by position. ו *and.* יהי *it shall be.* מבדיל *dividing*, particip. Hiphil of בדל. בין *between.* מים *waters.* ל *to.* מים *waters.* (7) ו *and.* יעש *maketh*, 3 pers. sing. fut. of עשה. אלהים *God*, nominat. את sign of accus. ה *the.* רקיע *firmament.* ו *and.* יבדל *divideth*, 3 pers. sing. fut. of בדל. בין *between.* ה *the.* מים *waters.* אשר *which*, pron. relat., (*are*). מתחת *under*, prep. compound. מ *from* and תחת *under.* ל *at.* רקיע *the firmament.* ו *and.* בין *between.* ה *the.* מים *waters.* אשר *which.* מעל *above*, prep. compound. מ *from*, and על *above.* ל *at.* רקיע *the firmament.* ו *and.* יהי *it is.* כן *so.* (8) ו *and.* יקרא *calleth.* אלהים *God.* ל *to.* רקיע *the firmament.* שמים *heavens.* ו *and.* יהי *there is.* ערב *evening.* ו *and.* יהי *there is.* בקר *morning.* יום *day.* שני *second.*

1 Kings XIX. 8–13.

(8) ו then. יקם he ariseth, 3 pers. sing. fut. of קום. ו and. יאכל eateth, 3 pers. sing. fut. of אכל. ו and. ישתה drinketh, 3 pers. sing. fut. of שתה. ו and. ילך he goeth, 3 pers. sing. fut. of ילך. ב in. כח strength, noun. ה of the. אכילה eating, noun fem. ה the. היא that, pronoun fem. ארבעים forty, numeral adject. יום days, sing. for plur. ו and. ארבעים forty. לילה nights, noun sing. for plur. עד unto. הר a mount, noun. ה that which is, article. אלהים of God, חרב Horeb. (9) ו and. יבא he cometh, 3 pers. sing. fut. of בוא. שם there, adv. אל to, prep. ה the. מערה cave, noun. ו and. ילן he lodgeth the night, 3 pers. sing. fut. of לון. שם there. ו and. הנה behold, interject. (there is). דבר a word, noun. יהוה of Jehovah. אלי unto, prep. ו him. ו and. יאמר he saith, 3 pers. sing. fut. of אמר. ל to. ו him. מה what, pron. interrog. (is there). ל unto. ך thee, pronoun. פה here, adv. אליהו Elijah. (10) ו and. יאמר he saith. קנא to be jealous, infin. to strengthen the next verb. קנאתי I have been jealous, 1 pers. sing. past. ל for. יהוה Jehovah. אלהי God, in construct for אלהים. צבאות of hosts, noun fem. plur. genit. of צבאה, putting the former in construct. כי because, conjunct. עזבו they have forsaken, 3 pers. plur. past of עזב. ברית covenant, noun. ך thy. בני children, noun plur. construct of בן, nom. to verb. ישראל of Israel. את sign of acc. מזבחת altars, noun plur. of מזבח. ך thine, possess. pronoun after a plur. noun. הרסו they have pulled down, 3 pers. plur. past of הרם. ו and. את sign of acc. נביאי prophets, noun plur. before a suffix of נביא. ך thy. הרגו they have slain, 3 pers. plur. past of הרג. ב with. חרב the sword, noun. ו and. אותר I am left, 1 pers. sing. fut. of יתר. אני I, pronoun nomin. לבדי by myself, prep. with

suffix יְ *my.* וְ *and.* יְבַקְשׁוּ *they seek*, 3 pers. plur. fut. of בקשׁ. אֶת sign of acc. נֶפֶשׁ *life*, noun fem. יְ *my*, pron. suffix. לְ *for.* קַחַת *to take*, infinit. of לקח. הָ *it*, pron. fem. accus. (11) וְ *and.* יֹאמֶר *he saith.* צֵא *go forth*, imperat. of יצא. וְ *and.* עָמַדְתָּ *stand*, 2 pers. sing. past of עמד. בָּ *on*, prep. הָר *the mount.* לְ *at.* פְּנֵי *face*, noun plur. construct for פָּנִים. יְהוָה *of Jehovah.* וְ *and.* הִנֵּה *behold.* יְהוָה *Jehovah.* עֹבֵר *passed by*, 3 pers. sing. past. וְ *and.* רוּחַ *a wind*, noun fem. גְדוֹלָה *great*, adj. fem. וְ *and.* חָזָק *strong*, adj. (*was*). מְפָרֵק *rending*, particip. Hiphil of פרק. הָרִים *mountains*, noun plur. of הַר. וְ *and.* מְשַׁבֵּר *breaking*, particip. Hiphil of שבר. סְלָעִים *rocks*, noun plur. of סֶלַע. לְ *at.* פְּנֵי *the face.* יְהוָה *of Jehovah.* לֹא *not.* בְּ *in.* רוּחַ *the wind* (*was*). יְהוָה *Jehovah.* וְ *and.* אַחַר *after*, prep. הָ *the.* רוּחַ *wind* (*there was*). רַעַשׁ *an earthquake*, noun. לֹא *not.* בְּ *in.* רַעַשׁ *the earthquake* (*was*). יְהוָה *Jehovah.* (12) וְ *and.* אַחַר *after.* הָ *the.* רַעַשׁ *earthquake* (*there was*). אֵשׁ *a fire*, noun. לֹא *not.* בְּ *in.* אֵשׁ *the fire* (*was*). יְהוָה *Jehovah.* וְ *and.* אַחַר *after.* הָ *the.* אֵשׁ *fire* (*there was*). קוֹל *a voice*, noun masc. דְּמָמָה *of stillness*, noun fem. gen. דַקָּה *small*, adj. fem. (13) וְ *and.* יְהִי *it is.* כְּ *as*, adv. שְׁמֹעַ *heard*, 3 pers. sing. past. אֵלִיָּהוּ *Elijah.* וְ *then.* יָלֶט *he wrappeth*, 3 pers. sing. fut. of לוּט. פְּנֵי *face*, construct before a suffix. וְ *his.* בְּ *in.* אַדֶּרֶת *mantle*, noun. וְ *his.* וְ *and.* יֵצֵא *he goeth forth*, 3 pers. sing. fut. of יצא. וְ *and.* יַעֲמֹד *standeth*, 3 pers. sing. fut. of עמד. (*at*) פֶּתַח *the entrance*, noun. הָ *of the.* מְעָרָה *cave.*

Psalm XIX. 1–6 (7).

לְ *For.* מְנַצֵּחַ *the chief* (*musician*), particip. Hiphil of נצח. מִזְמוֹר *a psalm*, noun. לְ *of.* דָּוִד *David.*

(1) הַ *The.* שָׁמַיִם *heavens* (*are*). מְסַפְּרִים *declaring*, particip. Hiphil of ספר. כְּבוֹד *the glory*, noun. אֵל *of God*, noun.

EXERCISES.

ו *and.* מַעֲשֵׂה *the work*, noun acc. יְדֵי *of hands*, noun plur. construct of יָד. ו *his (is).* מַגִּיד *shewing*, particip. Hiphil of נגד. ה *the.* רָקִיעַ *firmament.* (2) יוֹם *day.* לְ *unto.* יוֹם *day.* יַבִּיעַ *uttereth*, 3 pers. sing. fut. Hiphil of נבע. אֹמֶר *speech*, noun. ו *and.* לַיְלָה *night.* לְ *unto.* לַיְלָה *night.* יְחַוֶּה *sheweth*, 3 pers. sing. fut. of חוה. דַּעַת *knowledge*, noun. (3) (*There is*) אֵין *no.* אֹמֶר *speech.* ו *and.* אֵין *no.* דְּבָרִים *words*, noun plur. of דבר. בְּלִי *without*, adverb. נִשְׁמָע *is heard*, 3 pers. sing. past Niphal of שמע. קוֹל *the voice*, noun. ם *of them*, pron. gen. (4) בְּ *in.* כֹּל *all.* ה *the.* אֶרֶץ *earth.* יָצָא *is gone forth*, 3 pers. sing. past. קַו *music*, noun. ם *of them.* ו *and.* בְּ *into.* קְצֵה *end*, noun. תֵבֵל *of the world*, noun. מִלֵּי *words*, noun plur. constr. of מִלָּה. הֶם *of them.* לְ *For.* שֶׁמֶשׁ *the sun*, noun. שָׂם *he hath set*, 3 pers. sing. past of שׂום. אֹהֶל *a tabernacle.* בְּ *in.* הֶם *them.* (5) ו *And.* הוּא *he*, pron. כְּ *as.* חָתָן *a bridegroom*, noun. יֵצֵא *goeth forth*, 3 pers. sing. fut. מִ *from.* חֻפַּת *chamber*, noun constr. for חֻפָּה. ו *his.* יָשִׂישׂ *he rejoiceth*, 3 pers. sing. fut. Hiphil of שׂושׂ. כְּ *as.* גִבּוֹר *a strong man*, noun. לְ *for.* רוּץ *to run*, infinit. אֹרַח *a race*, noun. (6) מִ *From.* קְצֵה *the end.* ה *of the.* שָׁמַיִם *heavens (is).* מוֹצָא *going forth*, noun. ו *his.* ו *and.* תְּקוּפַת *circuit*, noun construct of תְּקוּפָה. ו *his (is).* עַל *unto.* קְצוֹת *the ends*, noun plur. of קָצָה. ם *of them.* ו *and (there is).* אֵין *nothing*, adverb for noun. נִסְתָּר *hidden*, particip. Niphal of סתר. מִ *from.* חַמַּת *heat*, noun construct of חַמָּה. ו *his.*

JEREMIAH II. 4–8.

(4) שִׁמְעוּ *Hear ye*, imperat. of שמע. דְּבַר *the word*, noun. יְהוָה *of Jehovah.* בֵּית *O house*, noun. יַעֲקֹב *of Jacob.* ו *and.* כֹּל *all.* מִשְׁפְּחוֹת *families*, noun fem. plur. of מִשְׁפָּחָה. בֵּית *of the house.* יִשְׂרָאֵל *of Israel.* (5) כֹּה *Thus*, adv. אָמַר

hath said, 3 pers. sing. past. יהוה *Jehovah*. מה *what*, pron. אבות *fathers*, noun plur. of אב. יכם *your*, possess. pron. ב *in*. מצאו *have they found*, 3 pers. plur. past of מצא. י *me*. עול *of injustice*, noun. כי *that*. רחקו *they are gone far*, 3 pers. plur. past of רחק. מעל *from*, prep. comp. of מ and על. י *me*. ו *and*. ילכו *they have walked*, 3 pers. plur. past of ילך. אחרי *after*, prepos. for אחר. ה *the*. הבל *vanity*, noun. ו *and*. יהבלו *they are vain*, 3 pers. plur. fut. of הבל. (6) ו *and*. לא *not*. אמרו *they said*, 3 pers. plur. past of אמר. איה *where*, adv. (*is*). יהוה *Jehovah*. ה *he who*, article for pron. (*was*). מעלה *bringing up*, part. Hiphil of עלה. אתנו *us*, pron. comp. of את and נו. מ *from*, prep. ארץ *the land*. מצרים *of the Egyptians*, noun plur. ה *he who* (*was*). מוליך *leading*, part. Hiphil of ילך. אתנו *us*. ב *through*. מדבר *the desert*, noun. ב *through*. ארץ *a land*. ערבה *of barren plains*, noun sing. ו *and*. שוחה *of pitfalls*, noun sing. ב *through*. ארץ *a land*. ציה *of drought*, noun. ו *and*. צלמות *of the shadow of death*, noun. ב *through*. ארץ *a land*. לא *not*. עבר *had passed*, 3 pers. sing. past. ב *through*. ה *it*. איש *a man*, noun. ו *and*. לא *not*. ישב *doth dwell*, 3 pers. sing. fut. of ישב. אדם *man*, noun collect. שם *there*. (7) ו *and*. אביא *I brought*, 1 pers. sing. fut. Hiphil of בוא. אתכם *you*, pron. comp. of את and כם. אל *unto*. ארץ *a land*. ה *that which* (*is*). כרמל *a garden*, noun. ל *for*. אכל *to eat*, infinit. פרי *fruit*, noun. ה *of it*. ו *and*. טוב *goodness*, noun. ה *of it*. ו *and*. תבאו *ye come in*, 2 pers. plur. fut. of בוא. ו *and*. תטמאו *ye defile*, 2 pers. plur. fut. of טמא. את sign of acc. ארץ *land*. י *my*. ו *and*. נחלת *heritage*, noun construct of נחלה. י *my*. שמתם *ye made*, 3 pers. plur. past of שום. ל *unto*. תועבה *an abomination*, noun. (8) ה *the*. כהנים *priests*, noun plur. of כהן. לא *not*. אמרו *said*, 3 pers. plur. past of אמר. איה *where* (*is*). יהוה *Jehovah*. ו *and*.

חפשי *those skilled in*, part. plur. construct of חפש. ה *the*.
תורה *law*, noun. לא *not*. ידעו *they knew*, 3 pers. plur. past
of ידע. ני *me*. ו *and*. ה *the*. רעים *shepherds*, part. plur. of
רעה. פשעו *transgressed*, 3 pers. plur. past. of פשע. ב *against*.
י *me*. ו *and*. ה *the*. נביאים *prophets*, noun plur. of נביא.
נבאו *prophesied*, 3 pers. plur. past of נבא. ב *by*. בעל *Baal*.
ו *and*. אחרי *after (such as)*. לא *not*. יועלו *profit*, 3 pers.
plur. fut. Hiphil of יעל. הלכו *they walked*, 3 pers. plur. past
of הלך.

Job XXXVII. 1–8.

(1) אף *Yea*, adv. ל *at*. זאת *that*, pron. fem. יחרד
trembleth, 3 pers. sing. fut. of חרד. לב *heart*, noun. י *my*.
ו *and*. יתר *is moved*, 3 pers. sing. fut. of נתר. מ *from*, prep.
מקום *place*, noun. ו *its*. (2) שמעו *hearken ye*, imperat. plur.
of שמע. שמוע *to hearken*, infinit. to add strength. ב *in*.
רגז *a tumult*, noun (*is*). קל *voice*, for קול, noun. ו *his*.
ו *and*. הגה *a sound*, noun. מ *from*. פי *mouth*, noun construct
of פה. ו *his*. יצא *goeth out*, 3 pers. sing. fut. of יצא.
(3) תחת *under*, prep. כל *all*, adj. ה *the*. שמים *heavens*.
ישרה *he maketh to flash*, 3 pers. sing. fut. of שרה. ו *it*.
ו *and*. אור *light*. ו *its (is)*. על *unto*. כנפות *the ends*, noun
fem. plur. of כנף. ה *of the*. ארץ *earth*. (4) אחרי *after*,
prep. ו *it*. ישאג *roareth*, 3 pers. sing. fut. of שאג. קול
a voice, noun nom. ירעם *he thundereth*, 3 pers. sing. fut. of
רעם. ב *with*. קול *the voice*. גאון *of majesty*, noun. ו *his*.
ו *and*. לא *not*. יעקב *he keepeth back*, 3 pers. sing. fut. of
עקב. ם *them*. כי *when*. ישמע *is heard*, 3 pers. sing. fut.
Niphal of שמע. קול *voice*. ו *his*. (5) ירעם *thundereth*,
3 pers. sing. fut. of רעם. אל *God*, nominat. ב *with*. קול
voice. ו *his*. נפלאות *marvellously*, part. fem. plur. Niphal
of פלא, as adverb. עשה *he doeth*, 3 pers. sing. past. גדלות

great things, adj. fem. plur. of גדל. ו *and.* לא *not.* נדע *we understand*, 1 pers. plur. fut. of ידע. (6) כי *for.* ל *unto.* שלג *the snow*, noun. יאמר *he saith*, 3 pers. sing. fut. of אמר. הוא *be thou*, imperat. of הוא. (*on*) ארץ *the earth.* ו *and.* נשם *pour thou down*, imperat. מטר *O rain*, noun. ו *and.* גשם *pouring*, particip. sing. for plur. מטרות *rains*, plur. of מטר. עזו *be ye violent*, imperat. plur. of עזז. (7) ב *on.* יד *the hand.* כל *of all.* אדם *mankind.* יחתום *he setteth a seal*, 3 pers. sing. fut. of חתם. ל *for.* דעת *to know*, infin. of ידע. כל *all.* אנשי *men*, plur. of אנש. מעשה *work*, noun. ו *his.* (8) ו *then.* תבוא *goeth*, 3 pers. fem. sing. fut. of בוא. חיה *the wild beasts*, noun fem. sing. collective. ב *into.* מו *some*, pron. ארב *den*, noun. ו *and.* ב *into.* מעונות *lurking-places*, noun plur. of מעונה. יה *their*, fem. for ה, agreeing with חיה. תשכן *they remain*, 3 pers. fem. sing. fut. of שכן.

ECCLESIASTES IV. 9–15.

(9) טובים *better*, adj. plur. of טוב. ה *the.* שנים *two.* מן *than*, prep. ה *the.* אחד *one.* אשר *because*, conj. יש *there is*, verb indecl. ל *unto.* הם *them*, pron. שכר *reward*, noun. טוב *good.* ב *for.* עמל *labour*, noun. ם *their.* (10) כי *for*, conj. אם *if*, conj. יפלו *they fall*, 3 pers. plur. fut. of נפל. ה *the.* אחד *one.* יקים *will lift up*, 3 pers. sing. fut. Hiphil of קום. את *sign of acc.* חבר *companion*, noun. ו *his.* ו *but.* אי *woe*, interject. ל *unto.* ו *him.* ה *the.* אחד *one.* ש *who*, pron. for אשר. יפל *shall fall*, 3 pers. sing. fut. of נפל. ו *and (there is).* אין *not*, adv. שני *a second.* ל *for.* הקים *to raise up*, infinit. Hiphil of קום. ו *him.* (11) גם *also*, conj. אם *if.* ישכבו *they lie down*, 3 pers. plur. fut. of שכב. שנים *two.* ו *then (there is).* חם *heat*, noun. ל *unto.* הם *them.* ו *but.* ל *unto.* אחד *one.* איך *how*, adv. יחם *shall there be heat*, 3 pers. sing. fut. of חמם. (12) ו *and.* אם *if.*

EXERCISES.

יתקפו *they attack*, 3 pers. plur. fut. of תקף. ה *the.* אחד *one.* ה *the.* שנים *two.* יעמדו *shall stand*, 3 pers. plur. fut. of עמד. נגד *against*, prep. ו *it*, for *them.* ו *and.* ה *the.* חוט *cord.* ה *which is*, art. משלש *threefold*, part. Hiphil of שלש. לא *not.* ב *in.* מהרה *speed*, noun. ינתק *will be broken*, 3 pers. sing. fut. of נתק. (13) טוב *better.* ילד *one born*, particip. of ילד. מסכן *poor*, adj. ו *and.* חכם *wise*, adj. מ *than*, prep. *from.* מלך *a king*, noun. זקן *old*, adj. ו *and.* כסיל *foolish*, adj. אשר *who.* לא *not.* ידע *knoweth*, 3 pers. sing. fut. of ידע. ל *for.* הזהר *to be warned*, infin. Hiphil of זהר. עוד *yet*, adv. (14) כי *for.* מ *from.* בית *a house*, noun. ה *of the.* סורים *prisoners*, adj. plur. of סור. יצא *he will go out*, 3 pers. sing. fut. of יצא. ל *for.* מלך *to reign*, infin. כי *though.* גם *even*, conj. ב *in.* מלכות *kingdoms*, noun fem. plur. of מלכה. ו *his.* נולד *he was born*, 3 pers. sing. past Niphal of ילד. רש, *poor*, adj. (15) ראיתי *I saw*, 1 pers. sing. past of ראה. את *sign of acc.* כל *all.* ה *the.* חיים *living men*, adj. plur. of חי. ה *those who*, art. מהלכים *walk about*, part. plur. Hophal of הלך. תחת *under.* ה *the.* שמש *sun*, noun. עם *with.* ה *the.* ילד *child*, part. masc. sing. ה *the.* שני *second*, ordin. numb. אשר *which.* יעמד *shall stand up*, 3 pers. sing. fut. of עמד. תחתי *instead of*, pron. ו *him.*

A further exercise is added, which has the clauses divided with ordinary English stops, the proper names in larger letters, the prefixes placed as separate words, and the suffixes cut off by a comma above the line.

JOEL I.

(1) דבר יהוה אשר היה אל יואל בן פתואל. (2) שמעו זאת ה זקנים, ו האזינו כל יושבי ה ארץ. ה היתה זאת ב ימי'כם, ו אם ב ימי אבתי'כם? (3) עלי'ה ל בני'כם ספרו, ו בני'כם ל בני'הם, ו בני'הם ל דור אחר. (4) יתר ה גזם אכל ה ארבה, ו יתר ה ארבה אכל ה ילק,

ו יתר ה ילק אכל ה חסיל· ‎(5)‎ הקיצו שכורים ו בכו, ו הילילו כל שתי
יין על עסיס, כי נכרת מ פי״כם· ‎(6)‎ כי גוי עלה על ארצ״י עצום ו אין
מספר, שני״ו שני אריה, ו מתלעות לביא ל׳ו· ‎(7)‎ שם נפנ״י ל שמה ו
תאנתי ל קצפה, חשף חשפ״ה ו השליך, הלבינו שריני״ה· ‎(8)‎ אלי כ
בתולה חגרת שק על בעל נעורי״ה· ‎(9)‎ הכרת מנחה ו נסך מ בית
יהוה, אבלו ה כהנים משרתי יהוה· ‎(10)‎ שדד שדה, אבלה אדמה,
כי שדד דגן, הוביש תירוש, אמלל יצהר· ‎(11)‎ הבישו אכרים, הילילו
כרמים על חטה ו על שעורה, כי אבד קציר שדה· ‎(12)‎ ה גפן הובישה
ו ה תאנה אמללה, רמון גם תמר ו תפוח כל עצי ה שדה יבשו, כי
הביש ששון מן בני אדם·

‎(13)‎ חגרו ו ספדו ה כהנים, הילילו משרתי מזבח, באו לינו ב שקים
משרתי אלה״י, כי נמנע מ בית אלהי״כם מנחה ו נסך· ‎(14)‎ קדשו
צום, קראו עצרה, אספו זקנים כל ישבי ה ארץ בית יהוה אלהי״כם,
ו זעקו אל יהוה· ‎(15)‎ אהה ל יום, כי קרוב יום יהוה, ו כ שד מ שדי
יבוא· ‎(16)‎ ה לא נגד עיני״נו אכל נכרת מ בית אלהי״נו שמחה ו גיל?
‎(17)‎ עבשו פרדות תחת מגרפת״יהם, נשמו אצרות, נהרסו ממנרות, כי
הביש דגן· ‎(18)‎ מה נאנחה בהמה! נבכו עדרי בקר, כי אין מרעה
ל״הם, גם עדרי ה צאן נאשמו· ‎(19)‎ אליך יהוה אקרא, כי אש אכלה
נאות מדבר, ו להבה להטה כל עצי ה שדה· ‎(20)‎ גם בהמות שדה
תערוג אלי״ך, כי יבשו אפיקי מים, ו אש אכלה נאות ה מדבר·

ON THE POETRY.

Hebrew poetry has usually no fixed length of line, or rhyme at the end of the lines, and indeed receives very little help from versification. Hence it has to trust only to the higher and more real beauties of its thoughts, its figurative language, its depth of feeling, and its elevating sentiments. Habakkuk iii. 9-12 may be quoted as a fine example of this class:

" Thou didst cleave the earth with the rivers.
 The mountains saw thee and they trembled;
 The overflowing of the water passed by;

The deep uttered his voice, lifting up his hands on high;
The sun and moon stood still in their dwelling.
  By the light of thine arrows they (the army) moved on,
By the shining of thy glittering spear.
Thou didst march through the land in indignation,
Thou didst trample on nations in anger."

Sometimes the poetry repeats its thoughts very agreeably in a recurring burden, as in Psalms xlii. and xliii., where we meet with the following beautiful lines three times:

" Why art thou cast down, O my soul?
And why art thou disquieted within me?
Hope thou in God; I will yet praise him;
He is the health of my countenance and my God."

In some of the poetical books, however, the verses are more marked as couplets, in which the second line repeats in new words, or answers, or in some way balances the thoughts of the first line. Thus in Proverbs i. 7,

" The fear of God is the highest of knowledge;
But fools despise wisdom and instruction.
My son, hear the instruction of thy father,
And forsake not the law of thy mother;
For they will be a wreath of grace to thy head,
And a necklace about thy neck."

In an argumentative poem, as the book of Job, the couplets are sometimes agreeably varied with a triplet, which gives weight to the sentiment when used at its close, or at the end of a speech; as in chap. xi.,

" And thou shalt be secure, because there is hope;
Though put to shame thou shalt rest in safety.

Also thou shalt lie down, and none shalt frighten thee;
Yea, many shall entreat thy countenance.
But the eyes of the wicked shall fail,
And their means of escape shall perish,
And their hope shall be as a puff of breath."

This mode of marking the couplets by the arrangement of the thoughts is called the parallelism of Hebrew poetry. It is seen as well in the English translation as in the original. It is also seen in the Greek of the New Testament, when poetry is there introduced, as in Luke i. 46,

" My soul doth magnify the Lord,
And my spirit hath rejoiced in God my saviour;
For he regarded the low estate of his handmaiden,
For lo, henceforth all generations will call me blessed.
For the Mighty One hath done great things unto me,
And holy is his name."

Some few of the Hebrew poems are acrostic or alphabetic, having the letters of the alphabet in due order at the beginning of each line, or of each verse. These are Psalms xxv., xxxiv., xxxvii., cxi., cxii., cxix., cxlv., Lamentations i., ii., iii., iv., and Proverbs xxxi. 10-31.

OF THE PROSE.

From what has been said about the versification it will be seen that it is not easy to mark the boundary between prose and poetry. Many fine passages in the Prophets may be called poetry, even though they are not in lines regular enough for us to print them as such. Many parts of Isaiah are in what may be termed metrical prose, marked by the parallelism of the clauses which we see in the poetry. It would seem as if a Hebrew speaker naturally fell into such a style of delivery when his thoughts were earnest and impassioned; and he probably accompanied it with an intonation of voice. As an example of this we may take part of a speech by Jesus to his disciples, Matt. x. 24-27:

"The disciple is not above the teacher, nor the slave above the lord. It is enough for the disciple to be as the teacher, and the slave as his lord. If they have called the master of the house Beel-zebub, how much more his household! Therefore fear them not, for there is nothing covered which will not be uncovered, and hid which will not be known. What I tell you in the dark, speak ye in the light; and what ye hear in the ear, preach ye on the house tops."

But we also meet with passages in prose which are in the highest degree poetical, yet quite free from this metrical character. Such is the account of Elijah at Horeb, in 1 Kings xix.:

"And behold, Jehovah passed by, and a great and strong wind rent the mountains and brake in pieces the rocks before Jehovah; but Jehovah was not in the wind. And after the wind there was an earthquake; but Jehovah was not in the earthquake. And after the earthquake there was a fire; but Jehovah was not in the fire. And after the fire there was a still small voice. And so it was, when Elijah heard it, that he wrapped his face in his mantle, and went out, and stood at the entering in of the cave."

The sublime in writing can hardly rise higher. Perhaps no other instance can be given of a passage in which our expectations are so boldly and so slowly raised, and then are completely satisfied.

The Hebrew writers, whether in prose or in poetry, often indulge themselves in a play upon words, as in Jerem. i. 11, "I said, I see the rod of an almond tree. Then Jehovah said to me, Thou hast seen well; for I am watching over my word to perform it." Here the words "almond" and "watching" are alike in Hebrew. So in Psalm cxliv. 3, 4,

"What is man [or Adam] that thou knowest him!
The son of man [or of Enosh] that thou thinkest of him!
Man [or Adam] is like to vanity [or Abel].
His days are as a shadow that passeth away."

In Isaiah xxix. 1, 2 the word Ariel seems to bear two meanings in the same sentence, thus, "Woe to Ariel, Ariel [or lion of God], the city where David dwelt!" * * * "It shall be to me as an Ariel [or hearth of God]."

ON THE ORATORY.

The books of the Hebrew prophets were written for the ears, not for the eyes; to be listened to, not to be read. This is shown in the very language, which has no word for *reading*, except קרא *to call out*, that is, *to read aloud.* And these books usually are in the form of speeches, as Hosea iv. 1, "Hear the word of Jehovah, ye children of Israel;" and Joel i. 2, "Hear this, ye old men, and give ear, all ye inhabitants of the land. Hath this been in your days, or even in the days of your fathers? Tell ye your children of it, and let your children tell their children, and their children another generation."

Joel's description of an invading army is very fine: "There is a people great and strong, spread like the daybreak upon the mountains; there hath not been ever the like, neither shall there be any more after it, even to the years of generations and generations. A fire devoureth before them, and behind them a flame burneth. The land is as the garden of Eden before them; and behind them a wasted desert. Yea, nothing escapeth them."

But it is the book of Nahum which more particularly tells us that the prophet was a speaker, an orator, who made use of action and change of tone, without which, or some corresponding comment, that book can hardly be understood. Thus he addresses the Jews and their enemies alternately:

"Jehovah is good, a stronghold in the day of trouble; and he knoweth them that trust in him."

Then pointing as if towards Nineveh, he says in angry tone,

"But with an overflowing torrent he will make an utter end of the place thereof, and darkness shall pursue his enemies. What do ye devise against Jehovah? He will make an utter end; affliction will not rise up a second time. . . . . Thus saith Jehovah, Though they be prosperous and likewise many, yet THUS shall they be carried off and pass away."

Here a contemptuous action of the hand may explain the word "thus;" then with a change to a more gentle tone he addresses Judah:

"Though I have afflicted thee, I will afflict thee no more. For now I will break his yoke from off thee, and I will break thy bonds asunder."

He then turns towards Nineveh, and with angry tone and action declares,

"Jehovah hath given a command against thee, that no more of thy name be sown. Out of the house of thy gods will I cut off the graven image and the molten image; I will make thy grave, for thou art vile."

Then by an eager look, and by pointing, he gives a hint of the good news which is coming, and says,

"Behold upon the mountain the feet of him that bringeth good tidings, that publisheth peace."

And so through much of this book action is quite necessary to explain the words. In no other book of the Bible is action needed to the same degree.

APPENDIX.

The Author offers the following explanations of a few words which he thinks are not satisfactorily explained by either Gesenius or Fuerst in their Lexicons.

אברך *bow the head*, the cry of the Egyptians in honour of Joseph, Gen. xli. 43. From the Coptic ⲁⲛⲉ *head*, and ⲡⲉⲕ *to bow*.

אלגום *ebony*, 2 Chron. ii. 7; less correctly אלמג, 1 Kings x. 11. It is part of the rare products brought home in Solomon's ships on the Red Sea. It was used for musical instruments and stair rails. Ebony appears in the Egyptian sculptures among the valuable products of Nubia brought to King Thothosis III. The Coptic ⲭⲟⲩ *strength* may be the root of this word.

אפעה *the horned serpent* of Egypt, the *Coluber cerastes*, Isaiah xxx. 6. It has a small fleshy horn on each eyelid, and is well known as sculptured among the hieroglyphics. From the Coptic ϩϥⲱ *a serpent*.

אתם *Etham*, an Egyptian town on the route of the Israelites, Exod. xiii. 20; Num. xxxiii. 6. It is פתם in Exod. i. 11, having the Coptic article prefixed; and πατουμος in Herodotus, ii. 158. It is Thoum in the Roman Itinerary, twenty-four miles west of Heroopolis.

בהי *the great toe*, the name of a boundary stone, a natural rock of that form yet remaining near to where the Jordan falls into the Dead Sea, Josh. xv. 6. It gives its name to a person, Bohan the son of Reuben.

גב usually *a raised place*, or *a boss*, but also *a hole, a den*, and in Ezek. xliii. 13, *the trench*, or drain to the great altar on Mount Moriah, of which traces may yet be seen under the dome of the Mosque of Omar. In Chaldee גב is *the back;* and in John xix. 13 the pavement in front of the judgment seat is called Γαββαθα, גב בית, a court described in 1 Kings vii. 8 as at the back of Solomon's house.

דרום usually *the south*, but *the south-west* in Deut. xxxiii. 23; *the southerly wind* in Job xxxvii. 17. Perhaps the watery wind, and the participle of זרם *to pour down*, with the ז changed to ד as is not uncommon.

כוב *Nubia*, Ezek. xxx. 5. The country was named from the Coptic ⲚⲞⲨⲂ *gold*, from the mines on the coast near to Berenice Panchrysos. This Egyptian word may have been also spelt Gnoub, as Eratosthenes has the name Gnubus *golden*, Hence while one nation dropped one letter, the Hebrews dropped the other from that word.

ליש *a panther*, mentioned with the lion and other African animals in Isaiah xxx. 6. In Job iv. 11 it is figurative of Egypt. From the Coptic ⲖⲈⲨϨⲈ *strong;* and hence in Prov. xxx. 30 it is said to be the strongest among beasts. This name probably covered both the *Felis pardus*, the panther, and the *Felis leopardus*, the leopard; and when the Romans hunted the lion and the panther in the amphitheatre, both the above African animals probably came under that name, Livy, xxxix. 22.

מוצאים *drainage*, Ezek. xlvii. 9, where the Dead Sea is called the Sea of the Drainage. The same as מוצאות, 2 Kings x. 27.

APPENDIX. 59

נא אמון *Thebes* in Upper Egypt, the Great city of Amun, *Diospolis magna*, Nah. iii. 8; so called to distinguish it from *Diospolis parva*, a city in Lower Egypt. From the Coptic ⲚⲀⲀ *great*, and Amun, the name of the god of that city.

סבא *Seba*, some part of Nubia, Isaiah xliii. 3, so named from the town of Seboua. It is also explained as Meroë; but the country now called Meroë was beyond the knowledge of the Hebrews.

סגן a *Sagin* or deputy, a lieutenant in the Babylonian army, Ezek. xxiii. 6; also a Jewish officer, perhaps a tax gatherer in the service of the Babylonians in Judea, Isaiah xli. 25, and in the service of the Persians, Ezra ix. 2.

סין the city of *Sais*, Ezek. xxx. 15, where it is called the Strength of Egypt. It had become the capital of the country about B.C. 700.

סינים the *Sinites*, Isaiah xlix. 12. The land of the Sinites is perhaps India, named after the river Sinde or Indus.

סכות *Succoth*, or booths, Exod. xii. 37; Num. xxxiii. 5, the Scenæ of the Roman Itinerary, eighteen or fourteen miles north of Heliopolis, and forty-eight miles west of Heroopolis.

סלא the brook at the east side of Jerusalem, at the foot of Beth-millo, the castle, 2 Kings xii. 21. From שלה *quiet*, and the same as שלח *Siloah*, described in Isaiah viii. 6 as flowing softly.

עית *Aiath*, a town on the east of the Jordan, which Sennacherib passed on his way from Damascus to Judea, Isaiah x. 28; the same as עי of Jerem. xlix. 3, which was on Nebuchadnezzar's route; and the same as עיים of Num. xxi. 11, and xxxiii. 45; but not the same as עי near to Beth-el.

פי החירת *the bay of Hiroth*, or Heroopolis, Exod. xiv. 2. This gulf of the Red Sea had reached to Heroopolis, whose ruins yet remain; but by the time of Isaiah the upper part had been cut off, as a lake, by the sand, and is called the Tongue of the Egyptian Sea, see ch. xi. 15. The town of חירת *Hiroth* is mentioned in Num. xxxiii. 8.

צי a *galley*, or ship of war, as opposed to אניה, a ship of burden. In Num. xxiv. 24 and Dan. xi. 30 the צי is a foreign vessel from Chittim.

צלצל *the spear-fly* of Abyssinia, Isaiah xviii. 1. It was brought home by Bruce from that country with the name of Tsaltsal, and by Livingstone from South Africa with the name of Tsetse. It is also the *locust* or cricket, Deut. xxviii. 42. The steel spear of Job xli. 7 (xl. 31) supports one meaning, while the steel tinkling instrument of Psalm cl. 5 supports the other.

צפ נת פענח *Zeph net Phœnich*, or Joseph the Phenician, a name given to the patriarch in Egypt, Gen. xli. 45. The Coptic ṄT *who* may form the middle part of the name.

שחל the small *black lion*, the *Felis Melas* of Asia, Job iv. 10, where it is figurative of Babylon, while the lion is Assyria, and the panther is Egypt.

תאוה the *Tih* range of hills in the Peninsula of Sinai, in Coptic ΤΑΥ *a hill*. It forms part of the name קברות התאוה *the burial place on the hill*, Num. xi. 34 and xxxiii. 16. It is a place well marked by the Egyptian tombstones. In Num. xi. 4, 34 this word is taken as Hebrew, and as meaning *pleasure or longing*.

WORKS BY THE AUTHOR.

THE HEBREW SCRIPTURES
Translated. Three Volumes. Third edition.

THE HISTORY
Of the Hebrew Nation and its Literature. Third edition.

SHORT NOTES
To accompany a Revised Translation of the Hebrew Scriptures.

THE NEW TESTAMENT
Translated from Griesbach's Text. Thirteenth Thousand.

THE CHRONOLOGY OF THE BIBLE.

TEXTS FROM THE HOLY BIBLE
Explained by the help of the Ancient Monuments. Second edition.

CRITICAL NOTES
On the Authorised English Version of the New Testament. 2nd edition.

ALEXANDRIAN CHRONOLOGY.

HEBREW INSCRIPTIONS
From the Valleys between Egypt and Mount Sinai, in their original characters, with Translations and an Alphabet. Parts I. and II.

EGYPTIAN HIEROGLYPHICS,
Being an attempt to explain their Nature, Origin, and Meaning.
With a Vocabulary.

www.ingramcontent.com/pod-product-compliance
Lightning Source LLC
Chambersburg PA
CBHW071910110426
R18126600001B/R181266PG42743CBX00010B/1